You Don't Know What You Don't Know™

Terry Lammers's extensive knowledge of the mergers and acquisitions business, combined with his straightforward and honest approach, connects readers with the expertise they need to succeed in today's business world. His book is the perfect resource for the entrepreneur just beginning their journey and the business owner looking to retire. As an author and entrepreneur, I've spent my life striving to make a difference in the lives of others. Terry's book will have a positive and lasting impact on the industry.

—**Dr.Tom Hill**, Founder of theTom Hill Institute,
Author of *Living at the Summit*, and
Coauthor of *Chicken Soup for the Entrepreneur's Soul*

You Don't Know What You Don't Know dispels so many myths around starting, operating, and selling your business. Terry Lammers's wealth of practical knowledge, in addition to his vast experience, makes this book one that you'll want to keep in your library as a reference and resource. Navigating the path to business success isn't always easy, but why try to reinvent the wheel? Most of your answers will be all laid out in a simple and totally applicable style in this book.

—**Alvin Brown**, BSc, D.O.M.P., CEO and Founder of
The Centre for Healing and Peak Performance and
Author of *Journey to Personal Greatness: Mind, Body and Soul*

Terry has been in the trenches of buying and selling companies. *You Don't Know What You Don't Know* is a great resource for any business owner.

—**John Warrillow**, Founder, *The Value Builder System*™
and Author of *Built to Sell* and *The Automatic Customer*

Terry Lammers's book is FANTASTIC! Whether you are planning to sell your business, buy a business, or both, Terry's advice is spot-on. With humility, transparency, and straight talk, Terry literally guides you through every step of an otherwise complicated business buying and selling process. I strongly recommend this book, and I will use the wisdom so effectively shared by the author to guide my future decisions about buying or selling a business.

—**Brett Blair**, Life Coach and Author of
From Autopilot to Authentic

An outstanding framework for every business owner. In this engaging book, full of business wisdom, Terry Lammers packed the best insight and information I have ever seen. With *You Don't Know What You Don't Know* in your toolbox, you'll walk away with great value and understand the simple steps to get the best and most $uccessful deal for your business.

—**Tammy Fadler**, Keynote Speaker and
award-winning Author of *Finding The Pearl: Unstoppable
Passion, Unbridled Success*

I run a successful novelty company that generates more than $100 million in sales. It seems like everyone in the financial field claims to be an expert, but no one connected with me the way Terry did. He actually knew what it was like to build a company from the ground up, as I had. The Billy Bob Teeth Company owes a great deal of thanks to Terry Lammers!

—**Jonah White**, CEO Billy Bob Teeth Inc.

YOU DON'T KNOW WHAT YOU DON'T KNOW™

Everything You
Need to Know to
Buy or Sell a Business

TERRY LAMMERS

NEW YORK

LONDON • NASHVILLE • MELBOURNE • VANCOUVER

You Don't Know What You Don't Know™

Everything You Need to Know to Buy or Sell a Business

Published in New York, New York, by Morgan James Publishing. Morgan James is a trademark of Morgan James, LLC. www.MorganJamesPublishing.com

Proudly distributed by Publishers Group West®

A FREE ebook edition is available for you or a friend with the purchase of this print book.

CLEARLY SIGN YOUR NAME ABOVE

Instructions to claim your free ebook edition:
1. Visit MorganJamesBOGO.com
2. Sign your name CLEARLY in the space above
3. Complete the form and submit a photo of this entire page
4. You or your friend can download the ebook to your preferred device

ISBN 9781636980829 paperback
ISBN 9781636980836 ebook
Library of Congress Control Number: 2022948263

Cover Design by:
Chris Treccani
www.3dogcreative.net

Interior Design by:
Christopher Kirk
www.GFSstudio.com

Morgan James is a proud partner of Habitat for Humanity Peninsula and Greater Williamsburg. Partners in building since 2006.

Get involved today! Visit: www.morgan-james-publishing.com/giving-back

I dedicate this book to my family, whose unique qualities have made my journey through life possible.
To my dad, who taught me about hard work and had the vision to let me be a leader.
To my mom who, although we did not always work together well, was the greatest mom I could have had. From her I learned to keep business and family separate.
To my sister: the older we get the closer we get.
To my wife who, although she does not always like my business ambitions, always supports me 100%.
And finally, to my children, Sydney, Caitlin, and Trent, who continue to impress and inspire me.

TABLE OF CONTENTS

INTRODUCTION

We were locked in the conference room. Mike, my CPA, slammed down the phone and said, "The son-of-a-gun will not budge!"

How could this be happening? Negotiating the purchase price was supposed to be the hard part, not this. The sales contract was written, the closing date was set, and we were hung up on the allocation of assets. How could the seller's CPA squash this deal at the last minute? This was my largest acquisition to date and the most complicated from a banking perspective. The way we laid out the allocation of assets was going to cost the seller over a $100,000 in taxes, but it was the only way the bank would accept the deal.

"What are we going to do?" Mike asked.

"I am going to make a phone call," I said.

I came out of the conference room with a huff, and the office staff snapped back to their desks. They knew I was mad because they overheard the talk in the conference room. I stomped into my office and shut the door. It was time to have a come-to-Jesus talk with Jerry, the owner of the company we were trying to buy.

Jerry answered the phone in his typical fashion, "Hey Ter, what's going on?"

This was the second trip to the altar for us in terms of trying to get this deal done. Jerry wanted to retire, and I needed his facilities.

"Jerry, we have to talk," I said. The conversation only lasted a couple of minutes.

Back to the conference room, I shut the door and sat across from Mike.

"Well?" Mike said.

"Run the numbers like we have them," I said. "We're good to go!"

MEET TERRY LAMMERS

I grew up in a small town in southern Illinois called Pierron, about thirty miles east of Saint Louis, Missouri. Pierron boasts about six hundred people. It is the type of town where nobody locks their doors and everybody knows everybody. Both of my parents came from hard-working German families, so in our family, no one sat around for long. There was always work to do.

After his tour in Vietnam, my dad grew tired of his work at the GM auto plant in Saint Louis and got a job as a tank wagon driver for Pierron Oil Company. A tank wagon is a truck with a tank on it that. In those days they held about 1,500 gallons and had four or five different compartments for gasoline and diesel fuel. This is what eventually brought our family to Pierron. By 1975, my dad had saved enough to purchase Pierron Oil Company, an act that sealed my fate in the oil business. Eventually, he built a new office for the company, which included a grocery store, a warehouse, and a shop area where workers could change tires, oil, batteries, and more. As a boy, I stocked shelves, changed tires, loaded trucks, swept bays, and did a variety of endless chores. By the time I was sixteen, I was behind the wheel of a tank wagon myself and made deliveries after school. I even made trips into Saint Louis to pick up bulk motor oil. As a father of three kids who are driving age now, it is hard to believe I was trusted to drive a large truck into the big city at such a young age!

I never cared much for academics. I could not wait to get out of high school, and I even graduated a semester early so I could work full-time at the company. Academics weren't my thing, but I recognized the need to continue my education, so I enrolled in business school to learn accounting. After I earned my certificate, my father and I decided that I should work outside the family business for a while. It would be good for me to try new things, meet new people, and have a different kind of work experience.

My first job was as a bookkeeper for the Rotary Club of Saint Louis. This experience connected me with a lot of the movers and shakers in Saint Louis, which proved valuable down the road. We hosted a weekly meeting for over two hundred people, so while on paper I gained experience in accounting, the most important thing I learned was how to stay organized. I helped coordinate the weekly luncheons, lined up guest speakers, assigned guests to the head table, and stayed on top of all the last-minute details and unexpected problems that came up during the event planning process. I quickly learned that this job wasn't going to become a career. It was clear I needed a better education and a job with more upside potential, and after two years, I decided to leave.

I enrolled at Webster University and took night classes until I graduated with a bachelor's degree in business in 1992. I also took a position with Mercantile Bank in their credit card finance division. While I only worked at Mercantile for one year, the experience I gained there was invaluable. I was part of a group of three people that did the forecasting, budgeting, and reporting for their $500 million credit card portfolio. The best part was that I worked with some very intelligent men and women. It opened my eyes about how a large company operated, which was quite an education for a small-town kid like me.

By 1991, our family oil business had some financial challenges. In the early 1990s, mom and pop gas stations were abundant. They typically included a shop that was staffed with at least two mechanics and full-service gasoline islands. They kept their money in the local communities and were the backbone of consistent cash flow for our oil company. But these local shops were quickly replaced by today's more modern convenience stores. As they went out of business one by one, our oil company's primary source of revenue became agricultural. This was good for business, but it was primarily seasonal, which left us with inconsistent cash flow.

We came across an opportunity to purchase Bone Oil Company. The owner wanted to retire, and it was now or never. I knew that if we bought it, it would put our company back in the black. It would also give me the opportunity to come back to the family business. Still, I knew it would be a monumental challenge because at the time, our company was not bankable.

In November of 1991, at barely twenty-one years old, I quit my banker's job and went back into the oil business. My commute was barely two blocks from my house, and my starting salary was $0 per year. My mom and dad made my car payments, and I took some money from the petty cash fund for the weekends. I laugh when I tell people that when I came back to work at the oil company, it was just me, my mom, my dad, and two trucks. And it was a good day if both trucks started! When I returned to the family business, our year-to-date sales were about $750,000. In future years, we would achieve that volume of sales in just three days!

The turnaround began slowly. Six months after I left the bank, we purchased Bone Oil Company, and our new company became Tri-County Petroleum. It was a Contract for Deed purchase with 100% owner financing. It was my first acquisition, and it was very successful. With the new company under our wing, we became profitable again, which set us up for future growth. Little did I know that this experience would give me the skills I would need for my future: working with attorneys and bankers and managing cash flow, overhead, the business transition, and so much more. We purchased another company in 1995 and then another in 1996, and in 2000, we purchased three companies. After that, we were off to the races. We pretty much purchased a company or built a bulk plant every year until I sold the company to Growmark, Inc. and eight of its FS member companies in 2010.

During this time period, we had acquired eleven companies and also developed and trademarked of our own brand of lubricants. What had started with just the three of us grew into a company with twenty-three employees, a fleet of modern trucks, and a service area that covered fourteen counties throughout southern Illinois and the Saint Louis metropolitan area. Sales eventually topped out at over $42,000,000 a year. It was a wild ride!

While we were always profitable, it wasn't a lot of fun to own a company with over 3,000 local customers when fuel prices peaked at over $4.00 per gallon. Truth be told, it was as stressful as it was thrilling, which was one of the reasons I eventually decided to sell the company.

One of my deepest joys was that I got to work with my father. I am proud of all we accomplished together, and I have the utmost respect for him. In 1996, he suffered a heart attack, and he decided to leave the company. Our family business just wasn't the same without him, which played a part in my decision to sell.

After the sale, for about three years I worked as a commercial loan officer for a large bank that had over 20,000 employees. And in 2014, my business partner, Dave Kunkel, and I started Innovative Business Advisors. I also earned my CVA designation as a certified valuation analyst.

Innovative Business Advisors handles mergers and acquisitions (M&A) work. We help people buy and sell businesses. We also do business valuations and consult with business owners who want to increase the value of their companies to make them more marketable for when it is time for the owner to exit the business. Our business gives us the opportunity to buy other companies that interest us, like the property management company we purchased in 2015. Life is never dull, and every day we learn and grow and change.

I have had the opportunity to serve on many boards and work with some great organizations that have influenced me both personally and professionally. One position in particular has had a profound effect on the way I approach life and business. For twenty-two years, I was a volunteer fireman with the Highland–Pierron Fire Department. When you live in a small town, there's no paid fire department. When the firehouse tones go off, you drop what you are doing to go help someone in the community, whether it is a sick call, a car accident, or a fire. There are so many decisions that have to be made at the snap of a finger. There are no meetings or briefings; you rely on your experience and training to get the job done. If you do something wrong, you learn from it and do it right the next time.

I worked next to the firehouse and lived just two blocks away during most of my career as a firefighter. I was often the first one out of the firehouse with the pumper or emergency truck. When you pull up to a fire, especially in a rural department, there's no one to give you directions, and every action is critical to the ultimate outcome. Every decision is made on instinct.

My years at the fire department taught me a lot—even about running a business. It taught me to read situations quickly, trust my instincts and experience, and make a decision. We grew Tri-County Petroleum quickly because we could assess any situation, make a decision, and move on. If something did not work, we figured out how to fix it, took the next steps, and moved on.

Another hard lesson I learned at the fire department is that death is inevitable. No one plans to die. Whether it is from a car accident, sickness, or a tragic fire, none of the people I encountered in my firefighting career planned to die that day. That lesson stuck with me, and I decided to live every day to the fullest, both personally and professionally. I encourage you to do the same. If you don't like your situation, change it. Life is too short not to love it.

I wanted to write this book to give someone who wants to buy or sell a company a down-to-earth, funny, real-life account of what it takes to grow and sell a company, as well as a picture of what life looks like afterward.

I wanted to write this book to give someone who wants to buy or sell a company a down-to-earth, funny, real-life account of what it takes to grow and sell a company, as well as a picture of what life looks like afterward. I have confidence in my work, and I don't have any regrets, but if I had the chance to do it all again I would certainly do some things differently. I hope that by sharing my experiences, you'll be able to make more informed and wiser decisions than I did the first time. Remember: You don't know what you don't know. The insights I share with you come from hard-earned personal experience. I think that is important.

I'll walk you through each step, chapter by chapter, to provide you with insights into the tools you need and the professionals you want to have by your side as you start, build, and eventually sell your company. Whatever your situation is right now, I wish you the best of luck, and I hope this book provides you with guidance and encouragement for your future endeavors.

God Bless!

Chapter 1:

WHY BUY AN EXISTING COMPANY?

I t is tough to build a business, and even tougher to build one from scratch. I did this recently with Innovative Business Advisors, and I now have a whole new respect for the challenge. It took several months just to create our website, not to mention completing all the paperwork and forms needed to establish and run the company. We worked hard to get that first client, oftentimes working for less than our normal fees. We created a marketing plan and paid for promotional materials. This is an expensive process and if you, like me, are not naturally a marketing person, it can be an exercise in frustration.

This chapter outlines all the advantages of buying an existing company and tells you how to maximize your competitive edge with your purchase. The first priority is established cash flow. Throughout this book we will talk a lot about cash flow. Cash flow is the beating heart of any business. Notice I use the term *cash flow* as opposed to *net income* or *sales* as my measuring stick—but we'll talk more about that in another chapter.

Improved Cash Flow

When you buy an existing company, you are buying their established business relationships and their current cash flow. It also means that you acquire the employees, customers, and associated equipment. It is likely that you will find immediate opportunities to grow the business. These opportunities may require additional capital investment, and you have the option to put new money into the business or wait until the company produces enough income to fund that opportunity.

In my experience, the company you want to purchase probably doesn't run at 100% efficiency, so whatever improvements you make will immediately increase cash flow. Even if it makes sense to increase efficiencies and improve cash flow immediately, I urge you to proceed cautiously. It is important to know and understand as many of the current inefficiencies and the costs required to fix them before you make your purchase offer. In fact, you may even want to subtract the cost of these improvements from your purchase price.

I bought a number of companies because the owner was about to retire. As an owner gets older, it is natural for them to curtail their investments in new equipment, to avoid new procedures, or to continue to use outdated computer systems and programs. These deficiencies often caused inefficiencies that could be leveraged to negotiate a lower purchase price. The costs to replace a complete phone system, decrepit computers, or outdated equipment can add up quickly, so be sure take that into account. Note that there's an important distinction between an existing business that needs some improvements and a company that is flat broke and running on empty. Stay away from the latter.

Sometimes, the employees themselves can be the cause of inefficiency, and you will need to assess their ability and willingness to adjust to your proposed changes. If you come in and want to make changes, will they embrace it? I have seen this situation go both ways. Sometimes the employees—or a single employee—will dig in their heels and resist change. On the other hand, they may welcome your improvements with relief. Be cautious in your decision to purchase if there's an employee who is unwilling to embrace change, especially if there is a chance that they could leave and take business with them or if their departure would severely disrupt the flow of operations.

To introduce and implement change can be a delicate proposition. It is important not to alienate any of your new employees. When I have purchased existing businesses, I ask the employees to keep an open mind. There's going to be a feeling out period where both you and the employees acclimate to one another. When you make it through this process, it can engender trust in you as a leader, particularly when the changes you make mean improvements in efficiency, cash flow, profitability, and more.

Overall, injecting new energy and efficiencies will give you a quicker return on your investment than if you started a company from scratch. This is why banks are very hesitant to lend to new start-ups. They have a high rate of failure, so most banks will not lend to a company until they have had three years of sales.

Gain New Customers

Now let's assume you want to buy a company that is similar to yours or is a competitor. Acquisitions can be, by far, the best way to grow your business. In fact, growth by acquisition was the key to my success. You often hear people say, "I'll wait for my competitor to retire or go out of business, and then I'll take their customers." That might work, and you may get some new customers, but you might also be waiting a very long time. And all your other competitors will be doing the same thing—waiting. But what if you paid your competitor a fair price for his business and, in the process, acquired and retained 95% of his customer base? Imagine how your cash flow would grow!

Acquisitions can be, by far, the best way to grow your business. In fact, growth by acquisition was the key to my success.

Most of the companies I purchased were my competitors. While I had an idea who some of their customers were, I did not know all of them. If I had waited for them to go out of business, I would not have been able to realistically find those customers, but when I purchased the company, I acquired their customer database and their pre-existing client network.

You may also work out a deal where the prior owner introduces you to his customers. He may ask them to stay with your new company through the acquisition process. And if the employees plan to stay, they can help keep the customers engaged and encourage them to stay, as well—which is another reason why it is important not to alienate your new employees.

Let me show you how this can work to your advantage. When I was working in our family oil businesses, one of the competitors I purchased had a refinery as a customer. They had held that account for decades, and when our sale was complete, they became one of our biggest accounts. The funny thing was that the refinery produced diesel fuel and gasoline, among other things, but they had to buy the fuel they used for their own operations from someone who had a motor fuel distributor's license, like us. They could not directly consume the product that they made. How could I have known that a major customer of ours would be a refinery that produced the very product we were selling?

Here are some things to consider in this example:

- We did not know the competitor had this refinery as an account.
- We did not know that they could even *be* an account.
- We had no idea they would contribute $30,000 to our cash flow.
- Even if we had known all of the above and wanted to go after that account, how would we have unseated it from our competitor? It would have been very difficult for us to get that business through a normal sales process, for the mere fact that you could not even get in the front gate, and the person you really needed to talk to was in Houston!

Customer loyalty is a big deal. Sometimes you can talk to a potential customer until you are blue in the face, and they will not make a change. They just don not want to go through the hassle of making a change, or they know the owner of the company, or they like their driver, or they are attached to the people in the office, etc. However, if you buy the company that currently supplies them and the previous owner endorses you, you have a very good chance of keeping those customers. In fact, we maintained at least 95% of the customers that came with our purchases. When I sold the company, we were still servicing the majority of the customers that came with our very first acquisition eighteen years before.

Recently, my partner and I purchased a company with several hundred customers. We kept the same management team, company name, and employees. In the past year we have only lost a couple of customers. In my experience, if you continue to provide a good product or service at a competitive price, the customers will stay.

Cross selling to your new customers is another big opportunity. If your business offers more services than the company you purchase, you can increase sales by offering those products and services to their customers. Likewise, if their company has services you do not offer, you can probably increase sales to your original customer base which, in most cases, is probably much larger than the company you purchase.

Reduce Operating Expenses

Acquiring new customers is just one example of the advantages of buying a similar company or a competitor. There are also plenty of opportunities to increase efficiencies in operating expenses. Think of all the fixed expenses you have. Those expenses will not change when you add a couple hundred accounts. Expenses such as your CPA, utilities, software, etc. most likely will not change.

I suggest you create a proforma that not only looks at additional sales and gross profit, but one that examines what expenses you can cut from their current expenses. Many times, when we bought a competitor that had the same territory as we did, we did not need to add a new driver. Another good example is insurance. When we purchased companies, no matter their size, the insurance expense would be over $10,000 a year because they had to have $2MM coverage in liability insurance. Since we already owned liability insurance, this was a big expense that we could eliminate. It often cost less than an additional $2,000 to insure what they had because we had already met those liability limits and had the minimum coverage needed.

Here is a classic argument you will hear when buying a company. Most people will tell you to only pay for the value of the company's *current* cash flow, not the efficiencies and increased profits you can bring to the company. For the most part, I agree with this 100%. However, we had an opportunity to buy a company that sat directly between two of my existing offices that were thirty miles apart. If we bought the company, the owner would retire, my current employees could easily cover his routes, and we could eliminate his office and bulk plant. But if another competitor bought it, they would likely keep his bulk plant and warehouse as a satellite location.

The asking price was about $100,000 higher than what we wanted to pay. But because we planned to essentially eliminate all his operating expenses, 95% of the gross profit from this operation would fall straight to our bottom line. We tore down his bulk plant, which kept competitors from moving into an area we dominated. In the end, we paid the extra $100,000, which proves there are exceptions to every rule.

Other Advantages

- Buying a competitor may give you access to a different · brand of products they sell in their territory.
- If purchasing the company pushed your sales volume over a certain threshold and you can get the next level price break on supplies, that savings will apply to the whole company. In a few short years, it could very well save you what it cost to purchase the company.

I have a friend whose family owns a chain of hardware stores. When I heard they had bought an old big-box store to convert it to a hardware store, I naturally congratulated him the next time I saw him.

He looked down and said, "Well it is kind of risky because it is not an existing store, but it is in a good area, and if our forecasts are correct, it will give us enough volume to start buying containers of product from overseas, which we cannot do right now."

Even though they did not buy an existing business, they bought a shuttered big-box store at an excellent price, and if their risk pays off, they will have saved significant money on the cost of goods sold for the whole company.

How to Approach a Competitor

The company that bought my oil company was my biggest competitor. I remember my first thought when they approached me to buy my company: *Are you kidding me? I have spent my whole life trying to take your customers!*

But guess what? They had the money to write me the check! They were a $6 billion dollar company. We had been in competition for years and had the same problems, concerns, and opportunities.

I often see owners hesitate to approach a competitor because the seller does not want to reveal their exit strategy. When an owner wants to retire or exit the industry and faces the challenge of selling the business, it sheds a different light on things. To ease this situation, seek out an intermediary or a third party that will approach the other company on your behalf. This can remove a lot of the awkwardness from the situation.

There are many reasons to purchase an existing business or to buy a company that is similar to yours. Remember to weigh your options, keep an open mind, and look for opportunities.

Check Yourself:

- What is cash flow and why is it important?
- What are the advantages of buying an existing company?
- Why is it difficult to start a company from scratch?
- What are some advantages to buying a competitor or a company that is similar to yours?
- Should you pay for efficiencies you bring to a company you want to acquire? What might be an exception?

Chapter 2:

BUYING A COMPANY

So, you want to buy a business. There are so many options, and it is a big bonus if you know what kind of business you want to buy. A lot of people have no idea what they want. They are just curious and are shopping around. If this is how you approach the process, it will be quite painful, and you will waste a lot of people's time.

How to Find a Business to Buy

A good way to start is to let your centers of influence—your banker, attorney, financial adviser—know that you want to buy a company. Believe it or not, my insurance agent has led me to several successful business deals. A commercial insurance agent is in continual communication with business owners and often have a feel for how long they intend to stay in their business.

Since you can find anything from a date to a mate online, why not seek out the business matchmakers? There are plenty of websites such as BizBuySell.com, MergerMart.com, and BizQuest.com that have hundreds of businesses listed for sale.

Since you can find anything from a date to a mate online, why not seek out the business matchmakers?

If you want a business broker, they typically have their current listings on their website. Something else you can do, which is done by private equity companies all the time, is to create a one-page document or email with a description of the type and size of business you are looking for. You can send this to brokers, post it on LinkedIn, Facebook, and Twitter, etc. Better yet, reach out to me!

Confidentiality

Let's assume you found a company that interests you. What do you do? First, find out the basics about the company. How many employees do they have, what territory do they cover, do they have any specific product lines, and will you need any permits or licenses to run that business? None of these things are confidential, so they are easily gathered. Go to the company website, talk with a broker, or even call the owner directly.

I am a business broker, and when I work with potential buyers, I make sure they are qualified to buy the company. I find out their financial strength, background, depth of knowledge about the industry, etc. As the potential buyer, you should be able to provide these answers before you approach the seller.

After you connect with the seller, the next step is to sign a *confidentiality agreement* or *nondisclosure agreement*. In a nutshell, this agreement means the information you receive about this company will be kept confidential. In other words, when you receive information about the company, do not run to the local bar and disclose anything about the business or what you know about their finances.

This seems like a simple point, but you would be amazed at how fast information can spread. This happened to me while I was in talks to sell my company. One of our buyers sent an email that ended up in an indiscreet employee's hands. Suddenly our phones started to ring, and our customers wanted to know if I was selling. This type of situation can be a disaster that leads to losing employees and customers alike. Fortunately for me, the sale moved quickly enough that it did not derail the transaction. However, if the sale had not gone through, it could have ended in a lawsuit. Be professional and keep your mouth, emails, and comments guarded.

As simple as this sounds, it can be a real challenge because you need to talk with other people to complete your transaction. Your banker and attorney all have employees who may be involved with the transaction. Most likely you will tell your spouse, but if your kids overhear your discussions, will they tell their friends? Confidentiality is key, and it can be very difficult to control. Remember, loose lips sink ships.

Financials

The next step is to gather the necessary financial information for you to establish a price or value for the company. It may feel uncomfortable, but you need to ask for three to five years of financial statements and tax returns. The financial statements are the face of the company, and they will often give you more detailed information than the tax returns. But you want to make sure that the tax returns match what is on the financial statements. If the company is large enough to have reviewed or audited financial statements, tax returns may not be as important. While the cash flow of the company is one of the main drivers for the purchase price, it is also important to find out as much information about the business as possible. Since it is early on in the talks, the seller may be hesitant to answer all your questions until they know you are in the same ballpark regarding purchase price. This is a valid concern, and it can be mitigated if you both agree on an acceptable *price range*, pending your due diligence.

In addition to financial information, there are a few additional items you need. The following is a short list of items that should be at the top of the list for an interested buyer. This is where you really need to do your homework. The devil is in the details, and these areas can come back to bite you if you do not dive in and discover everything you can before you buy. Every company has its weak spots, and if you do not ask the questions, you will not get the information.

Customer Concentration and Satisfaction

This is a big issue. You know the old saying that 80% of your income comes from 20% of the business? If that 20% comes from a very short list of customers, it should raise red flags. How healthy are those customers? How long will they stay in business? Will they stick with you after you buy? Are there contracts in place? Two years after I purchased a business, a very large client closed their doors and significantly reduced our business. Try to find out what the customer turnover is. Does this company have happy customers? Have they ever done a customer survey?

Equipment and Licenses

If equipment comes with your purchase, what kind of shape is it in? How long until it needs to be replaced? Have inspections and maintenance been done in a timely manner? How these questions are answered can affect the purchase price, since equipment failure and maintenance can be expensive. You do not want to spend a lot of money on equipment right out of the gate. Do you need to get certain licenses to operate the business before you purchase it?

Contracts and Intangibles

Intangibles are just that—intangible. You cannot hold them or see them, but they are valuable, nonetheless. Here are some questions to ask:

- What is the company's reputation?
- If they have a contract with a supplier, will that supplier transfer the contract to you? Certain suppliers may want you to qualify for credit before they will do business with you.
- Will the current owner stay on for a period of time to make sure that the customers transition smoothly with the new ownership?

- What about employees? Will they stay on? Are they in favor of the sale? Have the employees signed a non-compete agreement?

These are all very valid questions and, as I said, it is critical that you do your homework—what is called *due diligence*.

Financing the Purchase

At this point, if you need a loan, it is time to get the banker involved. Do you want to pursue owner financing, bank debt, or an earn-out? These are all are ways to get a deal done, and I have personally used them all. If the owner will finance a portion of the deal, it can often earn him a little more for the company, but it also creates a risk that he may not want to take. If you want to use bank debt, what sorts of assets does the company have that can be used as collateral? Will you need to use your personal assets as collateral or sign a personal guarantee? Ultimately, the bank's willingness to offer you a loan will determine your final offer.

Every loan can be broken down into two parts: cash flow and collateral. How much cash flow will the business generate to pay for the loan, and what type of assets do you have to give the bank if you cannot pay the loan back? Banks will typically hang their hat on the last three to five years of the company's financial information, and they will often have similar due diligence questions for the company.

Often collateral—or the lack thereof—is a showstopper for getting a bank loan. In other words, if you do not have it, you will not get it. If this is the case, Small Business Administration (SBA) loans, owner financing, or earn-outs may be the best options.

The SBA will guarantee up to 80% of some loans that, in turn, acts like your collateral for the bank. If you go the SBA route, I suggest you use a bank that specializes in SBA loans. They are much better suited to get through the red tape. Banks typically want 20% down for the loan, but some SBA loans only require 10% down. Sometimes the owner may finance that 10% or 20% as a note back to you. I have been involved in deals where the owner finances the purchase with a loan amortized over ten years, with a three-year balloon. That means after the third year, the former owner must be paid in full.

An earn-out is where the seller earns a portion of the purchase price, based on how the business performs after the sale. I have personally done two earn-out situations where we bought a distressed company and paid 25% of the gross profit for one year back to the seller. We did this because we were not sure if the customers could be salvaged, and this was a way to reduce our risk.

It is critical to have a good banker or broker when it comes time to navigate financing. Closing a deal can be very tricky, especially when real estate is involved or there's a real shortfall in collateral.

Tax Implications

Let's assume that you have a bank that will finance your acquisition. Now you can negotiate the final sales price and the details that surround it. Often the most difficult part is to determine how to allocate the purchase price to the company assets.

This can have huge tax implications for both the seller and the buyer. The seller will want as much of the price as possible to go to *goodwill* because goodwill is reported as a capital gain. Goodwill means that the company has value greater than the market value of its assets alone. Capital gains typically have a much lower tax rate than ordinary income. If a large value is placed on the *assets* of the company that have already been depreciated, it will be taxed as ordinary income at a higher rate. The buyer will want as much of the value as possible to be placed on the *assets*, so he can depreciate them and claim the depreciation expense on his tax returns.

Too often the allocation issue does not come up until it is time for the attorneys to work through the purchase agreement. It is best to get this worked out as soon as possible, and I suggest that you put these details in the Letter of Intent (LOI).

This issue came up with one of the companies that we purchased for over $1 million. When it came time to allocate the purchase price to the assets, we needed a certain amount to go toward the assets versus the goodwill, in order to support the collateral for the loan. The seller's accountant wanted a lot more of the purchase price allocated as goodwill because doing it our way would cost them over $200,000 in taxes, which was between 10% and 20% of the purchase price. That is a huge swing in what the owner expected to receive from the sale after taxes—and a very big deal. Eventually the seller agreed to accept our way of allocating the assets because it was the only way the bank would fund the deal. This is why it is important to have your CPA involved. When we talk about building a team of professionals to help you, these are the types of situations where you will need that team to help you through the transition.

Letter of Intent

A Letter of Intent (LOI) is pretty simple: it is nothing more than putting on paper or in an email how you expect to purchase the company. It should include what you have agreed to pay for the company, the terms of the deal, and how the purchase will be financed. Include which assets go with the company (equipment, names, patents, phone numbers, real estate, etc.), including the associated values for the assets. A good LOI will also list an anticipated closing date and how long the current owner has to stick around.

An LOI puts everything in writing that you and the seller have negotiated and agreed upon. It is typical for both parties to sign this document, and it becomes the basis of what your attorney will use to draft a purchase agreement. Most LOIs are simple documents that are one or two pages long, in bullet point fashion.

The Purchase Agreement

The purchase agreement is the last obstacle to closing a deal. Hopefully, your attorney has experience with M&A transactions. I have used the same attorney in 99% of my deals, and he works well with the other side, advises me about what is worth fighting for, what does not matter, how to improve the agreement, and how to get the deal done. Fortunately, I have never had an acquisition litigated due to the purchase agreement.

Your attorney will take that simple one- or two-page LOI and turn it into a purchase agreement. I have seen business brokers offer to do the purchase agreement on a boilerplate form, but that is a bad idea. Hire a professional to get the best results. Your attorney is there to protect you, but their opinion should not be gospel. Make sure to use your business common sense.

Of course, the seller will have their own attorney who is also looking out for their best interests, and there can be interesting dynamics between your attorney and theirs. I recently walked through an acquisition where, I swear, the attorneys were *trying* to create ways to screw it up. On another recent acquisition, the two attorneys could not have worked together any better and were instrumental in the deal's completion. The attorneys are there for each of you to make sure the i's are dotted and the t's are crossed. They should help you close the deal, not take the deal over as if it is theirs. The first case ended in huge legal fees for both sides. In the second case, the fees were fair and kept to a minimum.

The Closing

When both sides have signed the purchase agreement, a closing date can be set. The time between signing the purchase agreement and the closing date can vary greatly. Sometimes the purchase agreement is not signed until the day of closing. This is not unusual, but it can make that day more stressful because some of the details have to be hashed out at the last minute. Or the purchase agreement may be signed a couple weeks in advance, and everyone waits until the closing day when the final papers are signed, and the deal is completed.

If there is no real estate in the deal, this can be a remarkably unceremonious event. When we sold Tri-County Petroleum Company, it was just my wife, our attorney, and me in an office. All we had to do was signed a few documents, despite the fact that it was a several million-dollar deal that involved nine different companies. On the other hand, I have been involved in acquisitions that had champagne toasts, pictures of the parties exchanging keys, presentations of company paraphernalia, and more. The biggest part is when the money is exchanged, but these days even this is anticlimactic because most of the time it is done electronically, and you do not even get a check.

I do not want to oversimplify the closing date. You may have everything settled and ready to go as far as the purchase agreement goes, but if there are loans involved, another set of documents is required for both sides. Usually, the process unfolds in a very orderly fashion. For the buyer, his bank's underwriting department needs to have the loan documents ready to go on time. On, or the day before the closing date, the buyer will usually sign the loan documents, and the buyer's bank will wire the money, often to a title company, where it is held in an escrow account. Once the money is in escrow in the seller's bank, they will have the seller sign releases on any loans they have with the bank. The assets secured by those loans will then be released to the buyer's bank.

There may be additional money in the escrow account to be used for inventory or other things to be paid for post-closing from the buyer. If there is inventory involved, it is typical to count it the night before the closing or the morning of—before any transactions happen that day. Finally, if you are the seller, the remaining funds will be transferred to your bank account.

If you are the buyer, congratulations! You now have the opportunity to start doing what you wanted to do in this whole process. You get to run the company! Now it is time to meet your new customers and transition the company.

Check Yourself:

- What is a great question to ask a current business owner?
- Why is it important to know what kind of business you want to buy?
- Who are the experts you need on your side?
- What are the steps of buying a business?
- When approaching someone about buying their business, what are some good first steps?
- What are the non-financial items to consider?
- What is the purpose of a LOI?
- When will the purchase agreement be signed?
- What typically happens on closing day?

Chapter 3:

WHAT IS A COMPANY WORTH?

Valuing a company is an art, not a science. A company is worth whatever someone else is willing to pay for it. This is called the *fair market value*. According to Sageworks, the definition of fair market value is: "the price at which a property would change hands between a willing buyer and a willing seller when the former is not under any compulsion to buy and the latter is not under any compulsion to sell, both parties having reasonable knowledge of relevant facts."

How do you determine the purchase price? What is a business worth, and how do you decide what your initial offer will be? There are three approaches to valuing a business:

- The Asset Approach
- The Market Approach
- The Income Approach

The Asset Approach

The asset approach is usually used for companies that are losing money or have closed down. If the cash flow of the company is less than the value of its assets, the company has no goodwill, and the company's valuation is based on the assets alone.

The price of the company is determined by the fair market value of the company's *assets*, rather than its cash flow. The owner will normally hire someone to value the assets, which in turn, becomes the value of the company.

The asset approach does not always mean that a business has failed. Take, for example, an agricultural operation. If a farmer has no one to buy the business, they simply auction off their assets—their equipment, etc. An auctioneer documents all the assets to be sold and determines a base price for each item. At the auction, the assets are sold to the highest bidder, which determines the fair market value of the asset.

The Market Approach

The market approach is similar to how a realtor values a house. If there is a three bedroom, two bath, 1,800 square foot house on one side of the street and it sells for $165,000, then the three bedroom, two bath, 1,800 square foot house on the other side of the street that is in similar condition is usually worth $165,000. The market approach is an uncommon way to value a business because most businesses are unique. They have different revenue, different types of customers, different locations, etc.

But there are exceptions to this. A company called Business Reference Guide publishes what they call *rule of thumb data*.

This data comes from people who report business sale transactions to them, and Business Reference Guide compiles that data into a general rule of thumb price range for those business types. The data is organized by the NAICS codes. NAICS codes tell you what type of business it is: a dental practice, lawn care, retail store, etc.

You can use this information as a sanity check to the income approach. What I mean by a sanity check is that it uses a *different* methodology to reach what is hopefully a *similar* valuation for the company. I recently valued an automotive repair business, and I determined its value from the rule of thumb data. It was similar to the value I had determined using the income approach. While not common, there are some businesses that have very similar business models, and you can compare and contrast the value of these sales to come up with an estimate for your purchase. This is not a bad approach. It just is not the most common way to determine a company's value.

The Income Approach

The most common way to value a company is the income approach, which means that the value of the company is determined by its cash flow. If the cash it produces is greater than the value of its assets, the business has *goodwill*. Goodwill means the company has value greater than the market value of its assets alone.

The income approach allows several different methods to valuing a company and, in general, they all have to do with placing value on the cash flow.

Capitalization of Benefits Method

This method *capitalizes* (or determines the value of) *benefits* (cash flow) by determining the rate of return that would be reasonable when you own that company. The example below is very simplistic, and I recommend you find a professional to help you value any company you want to purchase.

- The first step in this process is to collect three to five years of financial statements and/or tax returns.
- Next, have a conversation with the owner about any of his or her personal purchases or expenses the company currently pays for, or what income or expenses the company incurs that are outside of the normal day to day activity of the business. This is called *normalizing the financial statements.* For example, if the company pays for a lake house or insurance policies for family members who do not work at the company, you will want to add that income back into the cash flow. Or if they receive rent for assets that will not be sold with the company, you will deduct that income from the cash flow.
- In most cases, I add the owner's salary back to the cash flow. This gets you to what is called the *seller's discretionary income*, which includes all the income (cash flow) that goes into the company, less the normal operating expenses. It represents the income that can be spent at the owner's discretion. You will want to add the current owner's salary back in for two reasons: they may pay themselves well above what a normal salary

would be for that position, or they might not pay themselves at all.

- The next step is to subtract what you expect to pay yourself from the seller's discretionary income. The amount
that is left is what you will use to determine the value of
the cash flow from the company.

Do this for all three to five years of financial information
you gathered and take a look at that trend. Is the cash flow consistent? Does it trend up or down? If it has been consistent, you
can use an average of the years. If it is trending up, you might
use the last year's result or consider what that future cash flow
number might be. If the cash flow has trended down, how low
will it go?

I call this downward trend *the glider path,* and you typically see this when the owner has stayed in the business too
long and has lost interest in the business. The cash flow reflects
it. In fact, this was the case in a number of smaller companies that I purchased. In one case, the owners had a vibrant
business, and then they lost a big account. As a result, they
did not have as much income or cash flow, so they did not
make improvements or add new services, and they lost more
business. They stopped marketing and did not gain any new
business. They were still making a living but did not have the
income to update trucks, equipment, etc., so they decided to
sell the business and retire.

The value of the company had greatly deteriorated over
time. The cash flow slowly but steadily decreased, and the trucks
and equipment were shot. What was left to buy? There was still

value to the company, but not nearly what it was years ago. The value of the company spiraled down, like a glider out of the sky. It is a sad story, but not uncommon.

Assigning Value

Once we know the true cash flow of the company, how do we assign a value to it? You may have heard that companies are sold for a *multiple* of sales, gross profit, or net income, etc. These multiplying factors are found in the information you receive in the *rule of thumb* data, and they determine the value for the company based on a *return on investment* or ROI.

Think of it this way: if you buy this company, how long will it take you to pay it off? If you borrow money to purchase it, how many years will the bank give you to repay the loan? The answer to both questions is usually between three and five years. Most companies sell for a price that you can earn back what you paid for it in three to five years. At a three-year payoff, your ROI is 33%; at four years it is 25%; and at five years it is 20%. The smaller the company, the higher the risk, so the more you should receive as your return on investment.

If you divide the dollar amount of the cash flow by the expected ROI, you can come up with a value for the company.

Example:

100,000 cash flow / .33 return on investment = $303,030 in value for the company

100,000 cash flow / .25 return on investment = $400,000 in value for the company

100,000 cash flow / .20 return on investment = $500,000 in value for the company

Now we've got some numbers to work with! Do you feel empowered yet? A couple of things that will really drive you to reach a value for the company are:

- Can you pay yourself a fair salary?
- Is that value a bankable number, meaning, will the bank loan you the money to buy the company at that price?
- Is it an amount that allows you to pay for the company in a reasonable amount of time?

These are the sanity check questions you need to ask yourself, no matter how you came up with a purchase price.

Let's talk about those three points. First, I have not met too many people who say they want to buy a company because they have too much time on their hands and are merely looking for something to do. A buyer wants to pay themselves or receive a certain return on their investment.

Second, is the deal *bankable*? By the time you finish this book, you will probably be tired of this term. It is very important, but all too many buyers and sellers overlook this. If the sale of the company requires bank financing, it has to be a bankable deal. I have heard of people who want a million dollars for their company, but there is no way you could ever get a bank to finance that purchase. That is your first clue that the price is too high.

The third point goes along with the second point. If the ROI is so low that it will take ten years to recoup your investment, does it really make sense to purchase it? We will talk a little bit more about that later.

The Question of Capital

Something else that could inadvertently alter the value of a company is the question of capital: how much capital (or money), other than the purchase price, will it take to run the business? If the company has accounts receivable, inventory, or work in process, these will all be paid to the seller at the closing. This amount is completely separate from the price you pay for the company. However, the bank will certainly evaluate how this affects the bankability of the deal. It might make sense to pay $400,000 for the business, but if the buyer has to come up with an additional $400,000 to replace the inventory and accounts receivable, it may no longer cash flow sufficiently. Believe it or not, this happens a lot, especially with first time buyers.

Let me give you a couple of examples. I recently valued a manufacturing company. The owners figured a valuation that the buyer disputed, and they were unable to come up with an acceptable purchase price that both sides agreed on. This was a large company with good financial statements and steady, consistent cash flow. Under normal circumstances, valuing the company would have been fairly simple. However, the company had about $1.5 million dollars in inventory that was over a year old, and half of that was over two years old. It was perfectly good, brand-new inventory, but the customer it had been manufactured for had stopped purchasing it. There was no way the cash flow of the company would support purchasing $1.5 million worth of dead inventory, and even if that inventory was discounted heavily, it did not work with what the owners expected as a purchase price of the business. Now that is an extreme example, but it gives you a good idea of how critical this can be.

Here is a more typical scenario. We sold a company in a construction-related field. The company had about $100,000 in inventory, and due to the nature of the business, their customers typically paid in sixty days. The company's accounts receivables ran around $500,000. Accounts receivable and cash almost always go to the seller at closing, and at closing, the seller is typically paid for the cost of his inventory with a separate check. The seller then collects his A/R when the customers pay their invoices. This means that there is a sixty-day cash flow gap for the buyer, and they have to have the money to purchase inventory AND be able to pay salaries, bills, etc. until money comes in from new sales—sixty days later. If they have to borrow that amount from a line of credit from the bank, it affects the cash flow *of the deal*. And if the buyers' borrowing capacity is tight, it could affect the overall bankability of the deal, which may cause the buyer to want to lower the purchase price or value of the company.

Well, that all sounds pretty simple, right? Cut and dry, nothing to it—don't you wish!

Other Assets

What about the value of equipment, accounts receivable, cash, inventory, and real estate? How does that affect the value of the company? Those are all valid questions. Let's break them down one at a time.

The equipment or assets go with the sale of the company; however, if there is any equipment that is not used to generate cash flow, those assets should be separated from the sale. A good example of this could be a construction company that has an old bulldozer or grader they rarely use anymore but is still sitting around. The owner should not include that in the sale and should sell off those assets separately.

Again, the accounts receivable and cash almost always go to the seller at closing. There are some deals where the buyer gets the A/R, but that can get muddy. Will the buyer pay for all the A/R, or just the accounts that are less than sixty days old? If this is the case, you are discounting the A/R from its total amount. Then you have to determine how to settle up if the buyer collects on past due receivables that they did not invoice. It is much cleaner for the seller to collect his receivables, although as we established in an earlier chapter, there is always an exception to the rule.

Be prepared to see language in the purchase agreement that says the buyer cannot collect on new invoices from a customer *until the seller has been paid his A/R* from that customer first. If large receivables are involved with the sale of the company, this makes perfect sense. What if a customer that is a slow payer owes the seller $30,000 at the time of the sale? After the company is sold, what obligation does that customer have to pay the seller anything? Chances are he will prefer to keep current with new owner instead of paying his old bills, and the seller could be left out in the cold. If that customer has to pay the seller before any new money goes to the buyer, it helps ensure that the seller will collect their receivables.

Real Estate

Real estate can be the most difficult thing to deal with in the valuation of a company. Oftentimes the value of the real estate can eat up the value of the company. When valuing the company, you must put a *fair market rent* into the company expenses for the real estate or the building where the company operates. If you have to buy the real estate with the purchase, your fair market rent should compensate for a loan payment. Sometimes the buyer does not need the real estate, and it can be excluded from the sale. Other times, the company depends on the real estate to generate cash flow for the company.

How do you put a fair market price on a single-use piece of real estate? Unfortunately, there is no clear-cut answer to this. Every situation is different. It is not uncommon for an appraisal for the real estate and building to be greater than the value of the company, and you have to determine if there is enough cash flow from the business to pay for that asset.

Here is a situation I found myself in. I always referred to my business as a fuel company that also sold lubricants, which meant that the majority of our sales came from selling diesel fuel and gasoline, but we also sold bulk lubricants. Our lubricants business was growing, and we needed to find a much larger facility. I wanted to purchase another oil company that was a lubricants company that also sold diesel fuel and gasoline. The value of the company had declined to the point where the real estate and building were worth more than the company, but their bulk lubricants facility was exactly what we needed for our operation. We could easily combine our lubricants operation with theirs and still have capacity to grow by using their existing real estate and building.

The value of their real estate and building were greater than the value of the company, and the cash flow from the company could not support the purchase price of the property. However, it was a perfect fit for me. I could acquire the property and equipment for less than if I had built it new myself, and I would also get their existing fuel and lubricants business. Winner, winner chicken dinner! It was a win for me and for the seller.

Intangibles

For the better part of this chapter, we have hung our hats on cash flow as the best way to value a company. However, there are some intangibles we have not talked about yet that are very hard to quantify, but they may increase or decrease the value of a company in the eyes of the buyer. Let's talk about a few of them.

The first is *recurring revenue*. For example, a bookkeeping/tax return business will typically sell for a higher multiple or lower ROI because the clients come back year after year to have their taxes done by the same company. A downside to their tax return business is that it is very seasonal compared to the bookkeeping portion. People only have their taxes done once a year, while their bookkeeping is done every month. Compare that business to a home builder or contractor. There is no recurring revenue there. Once the home is built, they have to find another home to build. These types of companies will bring a lower value or multiple.

Another intangible that should be high on the list is the management team. Can the company run on its own, or is it dependent on the owner or a key employee to run the show? Is this person, as they say, the chief cook and bottle washer? This is very common in small businesses, and this type of company will not bring the same value as a company where the management responsibilities are spread out over several people or departments, which is much more common in a larger business. Which brings me back to my previous point: the larger the business the higher the multiples.

A Word to the Seller

A lot of this chapter addresses the "what it is worth" question from the buyer's perspective. But if you are a business owner who wants to sell your business in the next three to five years, I encourage you to find a professional to value your business now. Business owners often rely upon the sale of their company for their retirement. If you wait until you decide to retire to find out the value of your company, you might meet with disastrous consequences. Let me give you a real-life example.

... if you are a business owner who wants to sell your business in the next three to five years, I encourage you to find a professional to value your business now.

One day I received a phone call from a man who said, "I don't need to talk to a broker about the value of my company, but if I can have a little of your time, I'd like to run a couple of things past you to confirm my thoughts."

I chuckled inside and said, "Well sure, I would be happy to talk to you. Please bring three years of your tax returns and financial statements with you."

He thought that was great, and we set a date to meet. When he and his wife came to the office, he proudly handed over three years of tax returns. They did not produce financial statements, so they did not have those.

I asked him, although it was kind of obvious, "Why do you want to sell the business?"

He said they had owned the business for fifteen years, they were both sixty-three years old, and they wanted to retire next year. Their son worked for them but had no interest in buying the company.

I asked, "Are there any personal expenses that the company pays for that a new owner would not incur? We need to add that into the cash flow of the company."

He replied, "Oh no sir. Mom keeps the books, and they are as clean as a cat's meow." (I promise I am not making this up!)

So here I am with three years of tax information, and he expects an estimated value in the amount of time it takes to check out at Walmart! I looked over the returns for a couple of minutes. They owned a distribution company that sold novelty items to convenience stores. The company had about $1.5 million in sales and, with depreciation added back in, made about $80,000 a year. It was pretty consistent over the past three years. I confirmed that they paid themselves a fair salary and that their son's pay was fair.

After a few minutes I said, "Well, I think you could probably list the company for around $250,000."

He remained silent, kind of in a deep stare. I looked at his wife, who had been very quiet through this whole process and watched as a tear rolled down her cheek. She stared out the window.

"Ok, wait a minute," I said. "Clearly that isn't what you were expecting. Let's talk about this."

The owner said in a huff, "I thought that since we had over $1.5 million in sales, the company was easily worth over a million dollars."

I started to explain cash flow and its ability to support a purchase price when his wife interrupted.

"Our credit card payment each month is around $6,000," she said, "and that is for all our personal gas, groceries, house expenses, entertainment, etc."

Those were personal expenses that a new owner would not incur.

"Thank you," I said. "That is great. It adds another $72,000 a year to the company's cash flow."

That adjustment gave us $152,000 in cash flow, with an ROI of 30% ($152,000 cash / 30% ROI = $506,667 potential sale price), which created a value of about $500,000.

"Are there any other expenses that we can add back to the cash flow?" I asked.

"Unfortunately, not," she said.

"Well, that increases the potential value of the company to $500,000," I told them, which made them feel a little better. We talked a little longer, they thanked me for my time, and down the road they went.

I tell you this story because I think it is safe to say that this was a devastating afternoon for this couple. Their retirement plans took a big U-turn. Sadly, even if the company was worth $500,000, it was before income taxes, broker fees, etc. were subtracted.

If you depend on the sale of your company for your retirement, get your company valued now. Do not do what this owner did and wait until the last minute. Build your team of advisors so that you will know what your company is worth when it is time to sell.

Check Yourself:

- What are the three approaches to valuing a company?
- What is one method to value a company under the income approach?
- What must be done to the financial statements before valuing the company?
- How does A/R affect the value of the company?
- At what price is inventory sold to the buyer?
- How do you calculate a debt service coverage ratio?
- What are some examples of non-financial factors that would add to or dilute a company's value?

Chapter 4:

THE FINANCIAL STATEMENTS

I f you want to sell your company, buy a company, or want to get credit of some kind, the first thing someone will want to see is the company's financial statements. You can look at the assets of the business or its storefront, but the most important thing a buyer or lender needs to know is how well the company is doing financially. It is also very important to potential lenders and buyers that they can receive this financial information in a timely manner. The inability to produce financial information in a timely manner is a huge red flag.

There are three types of financial statements: compiled, reviewed, and audited.

The most basic level of financial statements is *compiled* financial statements. With compiled statements, you give your CPA/bookkeeper all the relevant information from the business, and they take that information at face value, which means they do not check it for accuracy. They then compile your financial statements. These financial statements should comply with statements on standards for accounting and review services (SSARS), but the CPA or bookkeeper has done nothing to test the accuracy of the accounting methods used or performed procedures that would ordinarily be done in an audit or review.

When you receive a company's compiled financial statements, it is always a good idea to ask for their tax returns, too. Tax returns are legal documents, and if the owners lied on them, they could be in substantial trouble. You could even take this a step further and get IRS form 4506T signed by the company owner, which you would send to the IRS to get a summary of what was filed. It is pretty common for banks to do this. Believe it or not, when I was Mr. Banker, we had a fairly large trucking company that gave us their tax returns, but the bookkeeper had never filed them with the IRS. The owner ended up paying some huge fines and penalties that almost put him out of business. You also need to know if the statements were prepared on a cash or accrual basis. Compiled financial statements are by far the most common, so be sure that you get accurate information.

When you receive a company's compiled financial statements, it is always a good idea to ask for their tax returns, too.

The outcome of *reviewed* financial statements is a signed statement by the accountant that says they are not aware of any changes needed for the statements to conform to the financial reporting guidelines. In order for them to obtain assurance of this, they will conduct some analytical procedures and inquiries before they sign the financial statements. Typically, your bank will ask you for reviewed statements when you get to the $3 million to $5 million mark in credit.

So, what does this mean? When I sold the oil company, I had reviewed statements. We used accounting software, and it generated the financial statements. Our CPA made adjustments from there. When the CPA performs the annual review, they want to know how that information is put into the system and if it is accurate. They may follow the flow of a sales ticket to be comfortable that the information is correct. They might call some of your top accounts that have a receivable balance to see if that customer agrees with that balance. They may do the same thing with payables. They will ask a lot of questions about how the inventory is counted and check to ensure that what you report for inventory seems reasonable and accurate for a company your size. If there is dead inventory or past due accounts receivable, the CPA may make adjustments to your financial statements to reflect such.

So, what is the importance of this? Although a review is not as thorough as an audit, you can be more reasonably assured that the information you receive is accurate. Remember that the CPA has to sign this report, and if he did not follow the accounting rules, he could lose his CPA license. Does this guarantee that the financials are 100% accurate? No! The CPA's report states that the accountant is not *aware of* any modifications that need to be made.

You can expect to pay an additional $10,000 a year for reviewed financial statements. So, what does it really mean for you to have reviewed financial statements? It is going to cost you a lot more money, and it is a painful step up from compiled statements!

Audited financial statements are the highest level, and the auditor issues a report stating that it conforms to GAAS standards, which are the acceptable standards in the United States. This is a much more thorough process, and the CPA will confirm through a number of procedures that the financial information being reported is accurate. This could be done by any number of means, including making inquiries of the owner and physically inspecting things like inventory. They may call clients or vendors to confirm what you report.

I never had audited statements, so I do not have personal experience with the process. With audited financial statements, the CPA issues an opinion that the statements conform to the GAAS. Oddly enough, if they do not like what they see, they can also issue an adverse opinion or a disclaimer of opinion. How would you like to spend all the money for audited statements and get an adverse opinion from the CPA? Kind of makes me chuckle, but I bet we could get some stories from a few CPAs. The price for audited financial statements will vary depending on the complexity of your business, but at a minimum, I would expect them to be an additional $10,000 more than reviewed statements.

Banks recognize three types of validated financial information: your tax returns and reviewed or audited financial statements. What does *validated* financial information mean? It means that if you get caught lying, someone's neck is on the line. If you lied on your tax returns, you could be fined or go to jail. If your CPA did not follow proper procedures in performing the reviewed or audited statements, he could lose his CPA license. Remember that report they signed? That is why when the bank asks for your financial statements, they want the tax returns as well, because they want to make sure the tax returns accurately reflect what is on the financial statements.

If you are buying a company and you ask to look at its financial statements, you will want to do the same thing. Keep in mind they may not match perfectly, but they should be close. Generally, the financial statements will have more detail than the tax returns. That is why it is nice to see both. If a company does not produce financial statements, you need to look at the tax returns.

Bookkeeper or CPA?

Let's talk about bookkeepers, CPAs, and CPA firms. I am not a fan of bookkeepers, so if you are reading this book and you are a bookkeeper, I apologize. But let's be fair: if you have a really small business, and you hire a good bookkeeper, that is great. It is certainly better than nothing.

The larger your company gets, the more experience you will need. I remember that as my business began to grow, my bank was not comfortable with me using a one-person CPA firm. They preferred that I move my business to a well-known accounting firm. This probably was not fair to my previous CPA, but it was the reality of the situation. I also had to switch firms one time because we started doing fuel hedging, and the CPA firm I was with did not understand the financial reporting requirements involved with hedging. There was nothing wrong with that firm, but they no longer met my needs.

Be Prepared

Remember how I said that the financial statements are the face of a company? When you ask an owner for his financials, and he can immediately produce up-to-date financial statements and tax returns, that is a good sign. It is like looking at a car for the first time and finding it clean and shiny. But if you make a request and the owner cannot produce them or they filed an extension, or if it is July and the only thing they can give you is from the previous year-end, that is a red flag. It does not look good.

When you ask an owner for his financials, and he can immediately produce up-to-date financial statements and tax returns, that is a good sign.

Timing is important, but you also have to be able to read the financials. Do the account titles make sense? For example, I recently sold a gas station for a business owner. On his income statement he had "sales 19," "sales 20," "sales 21," and he also had regular accounts such as gas, diesel, soda, etc. How is anyone supposed to know what 19, 20, and 21 mean? More importantly, how will anyone who is interested in buying the company supposed to know that? Of course, the owner knew right off the top of his head that 19 was groceries, 20 was lottery, and 21 was liquor sales. Which is fine—if you are the only one who is ever going to read them.

What about this category: Miscellaneous. Miscellaneous *anything* drives me crazy, especially if it has a value of $20,000 or more. That category needs to be broken out. But you could also have the other extreme: you might see an income statement that has thirty income accounts and fifty expense accounts. Some of those could probably be consolidated. Sometimes statements like these come from the CPA. If you ask the CPA why they are like that, they might say, "I don't know," or, "Nobody ever asked me to change it."

We all get stuck in a rut and let things get sloppy from time to time, but when it comes to showing your financial statements, look them over a little harder. Sit down with your CPA or book-keeper and ask if anything could be updated or changed to make them look better. You cannot change the *numbers*, but you can make them more *presentable*. Whether you want to apply for a loan or want to sell your business, accurate, timely, and readable financial statements are a must.

Reporting Methods

Financial information can be reported on a *cash* or *accrual* basis, and it is very important to know the difference. I am not a CPA, but this should give you the basics.

With cash basis accounting, you do not report anything until the cash has been received or spent. So, if you make a sale to a customer today and he does not pay you for thirty days, it is not considered a sale or income until the day you receive the payment. The same applies with payables. If you make a purchase today but do not pay for it for thirty, days it is not an expense until the day you pay for it.

In accrual basis accounting, the day you make the sale, it is reflected as a sale and is considered income. If you do not get paid for thirty days, you have an accounts receivable until the day you receive payment. Same with payables or expenses. The day you make the purchase, it is an expense. If you do not pay for it for thirty days, you have an accounts payable until you actually pay for it.

Why does this matter? It is important because cash basis accounting can allow a business owner to monkey around with the income statement. If you want to purchase a company and the owner manipulates the income by using cash basis accounting, those income reports can be deceiving. If the owner wants to show that the company made a lot of money, he could deposit the cash that comes in and not pay any bills. If they do not pay the bills, it is not reflected as an expense. Conversely, if they want to show that the company did not make any money, they could pay lots of bills but not deposit any checks. If they do not deposit the check in the bank, it is not income. And why would a company not want to show income? Because they are trying to avoid paying taxes!

If they are doing cash basis accounting, there will be no accounts receivable or accounts payable on the balance sheet. Without accounts payables and receivables, you do not know what is out there. What if there are many customers who pay in three to six months? What if this company does not pay its bills, and there are a lot of upset suppliers out there? You could be stepping into a mess. Be very skeptical if a business owner presents you with financial information that uses cash basis accounting.

And if you are a business owner who is reading this, and you have cash basis financial statements—stop now! This is a disaster waiting to happen.

It is not uncommon to see accrual financial statements and cash basis tax returns. It is not the worst thing in the world, but they are going to have to pay the taxes sooner or later. If you are doing this and are in the process of selling your company, hopefully your CPA can reconcile the cash basis to the accrual basis.

One more thing to watch out for. In a recent deal of a sale that I brokered, halfway through, the CPA firm switched the type of information they gave me. With some accounting software, you can switch from cash basis reporting to accrual basis with the click of a button. Suddenly they were giving us cash basis reports vs. accrual basis reports. I did not catch it at first, and the buyer freaked out for a day or two until we figured out what had changed. No harm done in the end, but we did not need the drama. You do not want to do anything that creates stress for the buyer.

Bottom line: use accrual basis accounting to report your financial information and save everyone a headache.

Check Yourself:

- What are the three types of financial statements?
- What are the three validated sources of financial information?
- What are the two methods used to report financial data? Which one is better and why?
- Why is the timeliness of releasing financial statements important?
- Why is it important to have good account titles on your financial statements?

Chapter 5:

HIRE THE RIGHT ATTORNEY

What kind of attorney should you hire to help you through the process? If you are buying or selling a business, you should hire an attorney that has experience in M&A transactions. Depending on the size of the transaction, he or she may need the help of another attorney. Maybe someone who specializes in taxation. There is nothing wrong with that. Just remember that you are the one who is paying the bill.

Speaking of bills, what should you expect to pay? Attorneys are generally paid by the hour, but there is nothing wrong with asking what you should expect the overall cost to be. Some attorneys will give you a set fee, and I have seen this for both large and small transactions.

There are a few ways to keep the costs in check. First, be as organized as you can. Get the information to your attorney in a timely manner, and make sure that what you provide is accurate, so they do not have to rework it or follow up. Time is money.

Second, make sure your attorney is not a deal killer. If your lawyer wants to argue every point, you are probably never going to get a deal done. Attorneys are focused on mitigating risk, and their job is to protect you. However, you need to make sure your legal counsel knows your tolerance for risk and how to choose your battles. Too many times, I have seen a client accept what their attorney says as gospel, and then dig in their heels because of it. Some things are not worth the fight, while others will be a clear "yes" or "no." You have to make your own decisions, and you should be the one who tells your attorney when to fight and when to leave it, not the other way around.

It is often cheaper to have the other side draft the asset purchase agreement and have your attorney review it. Less time on your side means less cost. That said, in my case I often had my attorney draft the sales contract because we had purchased several other oil companies, and the deals were all in similar format. I would tell the seller that we had done this before and let them know what the sticking points would be with their attorney. This was very effective and helped keep the ball moving.

It is often cheaper to have the other side draft the asset purchase agreement and have your attorney review it. Less time on your side means less cost.

In smaller deals, some buyers and sellers like to share an attorney and split the cost. This falls under the "don't make a mountain out of a molehill" logic. In situations where the buyers and sellers of a small company know each other and trust the attorney, this allows the deal to get done efficiently—and at half the cost to each party.

I have had a number of experiences with attorneys, and thankfully most of them have been good. There was one exception. With my very first purchase, the seller and I agreed on nearly every point, but the two attorneys bickered over every if, and, or but in the contract. We finally told our counsel that we planned to sign the thing that day and told them to get it done, which gave them about an hour to finish the contract. My Dad and I picked up the seller, and the three of us rode together to the closing at his attorney's office to sign the papers. This was before the Internet—back in the days when fax machines used thermal paper on a big roll. We signed a giant stack of curled-up paper and got the deal done!

Here is an example of how it should go every time. I represented the seller of a company, found a buyer, and the total price was just under $1 million. I also referred the buyer and seller to their respective attorneys. I knew the seller's attorney, so I knew he would do a good job. The business to be sold was in another town several hours away, so I asked around and got a few recommendations for the buyer, who was from another state and was preparing to move his family to town. I checked out the attorney's website, and this looked like a deal she could handle. I introduced the buyer to the attorney and had her prepare the draft of the sales contract. Even though this is contrary to what I recommended earlier, I knew she would do a good job. She even helped the buyer get the necessary permits and licenses needed to run the business.

Remember that these two attorneys had never met each other, and neither one of them knew their clients before this transaction. The draft purchase agreement was presented to the seller's attorney, who made very few changes. He presented it back in bullet point fashion. The two attorneys called each other to discuss how to prepare language where they had differences. Even in a small transaction, as this one was, there are always so many details that it is critical to have knowledgeable attorneys on both sides. We met to close the deal at the buyer attorney's office, everyone signed the papers, exchanged the money, and it was done. It should always be that easy.

And yet, it does not always go so smoothly. I was involved in the sale of another company where we negotiated a fair price with the seller and her CPA. When we were ready to write a sales contract, a partner of the buyer wanted to use an attorney he knew. The seller wanted to use her estate attorney from a large firm. First red flag: do not use an estate attorney for an M&A transaction. Second red flag: the buyer's lawyer had previously worked for the same firm, knew the estate attorney all too well, and they did not like each other at all. I voiced my concerns to both the buyer and the seller when we were in the same room.

"I have grave concerns about this situation," I said, "and I think it has disaster written all over it."

They did not see a problem.

The sale was a fight from the get-go. Neither attorney trusted nor liked each other, so the last thing they wanted was to work together—let alone make a change the other attorney suggested. The seller had never sold a business before, so she took whatever her attorney said as gospel. Even the seller's CPA was frustrated. There is no doubt in my mind that if the buyer had not known and trusted the seller, the deal would never have gone through.

It took six hard months to close on a company with a transaction value less than $2 million. And then came the bill! It was double what I had figured into the loan for the buyer, and yes, the attorneys expected to be paid in less than thirty days. For the sake of confidentiality, I cannot give exact numbers, but it was four times what I paid the attorney who helped me sell my oil company, and that transaction value was over four times what this one was. Did I mention that the buyer is still bitter?

Choose your attorney wisely. Choose an attorney that knows M&A and can get things done. While you negotiate contracts, use your business skills, and make sound business decisions. Mitigate your risks but choose your battles. It is refreshing to work with a good attorney and frustrating to work with a bad attorney. If it does not look good out of the gate, stop and run the other direction. Your wallet will be better off for it.

If you start to do business in more than one state, you may need to find an attorney who is licensed in that state, or you may want to find a firm that can represent you in both in states. Just like I had to change CPAs because they could not handle our fuel hedging, you may have to change law firms if you are not confident they can handle all your needs. You can also consider using multiple attorneys. Whether or not they come from the same firm is your choice. I poked fun at the estate planning attorney earlier, but if you grow your company and it is worth several million dollars, you will need the help of a skilled estate planning attorney. Not having one could cost you hundreds of thousands of dollars, even before you sell.

Your attorney is there to keep you out of trouble. It is a good idea to run your thoughts past him or her before you act. Case in point: we had a bulk plant with a four-bay, concrete-block building on the property that sat unused. We did what made sense at the time and leased it to a small business that used it as a shop and for storage. After we had been working together for a while, he stopped paying his rent. After months of unsuccessful attempts to contact him, we decided to take our boom truck, go to the local concrete plant, get four large concrete blocks, and place one in front of each door to block his access.

Your attorney is there to keep you out of trouble. It is a good idea to run your thoughts past him or her before you act.

The tenant never returned my calls, but his attorney found me after the blocks were in place. Shortly after that, my own attorney convinced me that I could not drop large concrete blocks in front of his doors, even if he had not paid the rent. I may not have agreed, but he did keep me from getting involved in a lawsuit, and he still laughs at me today for that episode.

Check Yourself:

- What kind of attorney should you have?
- What should you expect to pay an attorney?
- When might it be appropriate for a buyer and seller to split the cost of an attorney?
- Why might it be a good idea to have the other party draft the first purchase agreement?
- What is the purpose of an attorney?
- Who should ultimately make the final decisions?

Chapter 6

CHOOSE THE RIGHT BANK

A bank is a bank is a bank, right? It is amazing how far that is from the truth! I never realized that until I worked for a bank. When I owned Tri-County Petroleum Company, I worked with a big bank until, for various reasons (primarily a new credit manager who, in my mind, had a screw loose), I switched and split my business between two small banks. I am not saying small banks are better than big banks, but that change made sense for me. Credit unions can also be great to work with.

What are some of the differences between banks, and what should you think about if you want to buy a business, sell your business, or secure a loan?

Big Banks vs. Small Banks

Big banks are highly structured and government regulations play a large part in how they do business. If you apply for a loan from a big bank, your application and paperwork will go through an underwriting department. Other than entering your information into the system, your local contact has very little to say about whether your loan is approved. You lose that personal connection, and the underwriter does not know you. The smaller your loan, the more true this is. When you start getting to larger loans, if you have a commercial loan officer, you will receive more attention.

If there are no issues with your loan request, and you easily meet their requirements, getting a loan from a big bank can be a very speedy process. Why? They probably use a centralized underwriting process, which means that your application goes to a department—often in another city or state—that only processes loans. The underwriter who entered your loan application can also approve it or have their supervisor approve it, possibly on the same day.

With a smaller bank, the loan process is a bit looser. They will want and need most of the same information, but the person you deal with at the branch level—their commercial lender—will know the one or two people in the underwriting department who are responsible to approve or deny your loan. That commercial lender will likely have the authority to approve your loan, and he or she may even sit on the loan committee. They may know you and your family personally and they know your story and can make your case to the loan committee.

When you work with a smaller, local bank, you are likely to get a decision based on more than just your numbers. They may be more willing to consider your character and personal experience when they make their decision. I think this is great, but oddly enough it can also hurt you. If you do not have a great reputation, or if you have had personal issues, the small bank may choose not to do business with you just because they do not like you.

When you work with a smaller, local bank, you are likely to get a decision based on more than just your numbers. They may be more willing to consider your character and personal experience when they make their decision.

Everybody likes to talk about the good old days, when you called up your bank, and the president of the bank said, "No problem, we'll take care of that for you." That will not happen at a big bank. A few years ago, my parents sold the house they had lived in for over forty years to downsize to a condo. They needed a bridge loan to buy the condo while their house was on the market. I was working for a big bank at that time, so naturally they came to me for help. It would have taken at least sixty days for them to get a loan with me because we would have had to get appraisals etc., and I could not have done the loan anyway because the home mortgage department would have handled it.

My parents had not borrowed money in years, so they were confused when I told them to go to one of the local banks. I told them I would call the president of one of the local banks who had known my parents his whole life to tell him they were on their way. He laughed and said to send them right over. The loan was approved before they even got to the bank. Now, to be fair, if you need a $15 million-dollar loan, you are not going to get that small bank because that amount would be way over their lending limit.

Lending Limits

Banks have lending limits? Depending on the size of the bank, the government sets a maximum amount for any single loan they can make. Assume your local bank's lending limit is $10 million. Even if you come to them with a loan request for $8 million, they will probably be a little squeamish because, even if it is a perfect loan, that is a lot of risk for them to take. One of the banks I used only had a $2 million lending limit, which is why I had to use two banks: I needed a line of credit that was bigger than their lending limit. But it was always nice to call that banker when I needed $250,000 to buy a truck. He could approve it over the phone because he had the credit authority to do so. The main point is that the size of your bank should be determined by the size and complexity of your needs.

Specialization

When it comes to lending, there is one other thing to think about: what type of loans does the bank make? Do they specialize in a certain industry? Do they have industries or markets they will not lend to, such as restaurants or construction companies? I know a small bank that, for business lending, prefers real estate loans. If your loan involves a building or land, they are more likely to approve that loan. This same bank also likes non-owner-occupied real estate, which that the owner does not have a business in the building. A strip mall, for example.

Other banks will not make non-owner-occupied loans or will require that you occupy a certain percentage of the building. They may even require your company to make the loan payment on the whole building, independent of rent payments from tenants. Lending to attorneys can be a challenge because they do not have much collateral, but I know a bank that likes to lend to law firms. Sometimes banks have programs for specific market segments such as medical, agricultural, and construction.

If you are interested in an SBA loan, I highly recommend working with a bank that specializes in SBA loans. Banks that specialize in SBA loans can get them done in about the same amount of time it takes to do a conventional loan.

If you are a trucking company or you buy a lot of equipment, look for a bank that also offers leasing programs. Depending on your tax situation, banks can offer some high-quality leasing opportunities.

Who Is Your Contact Person?

Let's look specifically at loan officers or the personnel at the bank that will handle your borrowing needs. When you go to the bank for a loan, does the person you talk to understand lending? Or are they merely a sales representative who tries to get loans? It is sad, but when you talk to a loan officer from a big bank, you are probably just talking to a salesperson who knows what paperwork to get from you and really wants to make that loan, so he can make his goal. Most likely, he is inexperienced, and if he does have good experience, he probably has only been with the bank for a short time. It is amazing how much of a revolving door those banks can be.

If go to a small community bank, your loan officer has probably been with the bank for many years. You should be able to have a good conversation with them about their lending requirements and should understand how likely they are to approve your loan.

Other Bank Services

What about their other services? There is so much more to banking than just loans. What about checking accounts, deposits, online banking, and fees? Again, all of these things depend on your needs. If you are a small business and you only deposit twenty or thirty checks a month, none of this probably matters, and you just want a free checking account.

While I was working for the big bank, I had a client that deposited over five hundred checks a day! He had one full-time person, and all she did was work on their daily deposit. It took a lot of time to open five hundred envelopes, add up the checks, and make that deposit. In my opinion, they should have used what is called a *lock box service* where the customers mail their payments directly to the bank. The bank makes the deposit for you and sends you an electronic file that shows you a picture of each check and anything else that was in the envelope. A big bank can do that. It costs money to use that service, but not as much as a full-time employee. I could never talk that owner into using that service because he said he liked to walk past her desk and see that big pile of checks.

If you are a bigger company and you do a lot of online banking or have a lot of vendors that pay you by EFT (electronic funds transfer), you may need to go to a bigger bank. The level of sophistication will be higher, as these types of services are very expensive to develop and support. Smaller banks just cannot afford to offer these services.

Fees

Nobody likes to pay fees, right? Well, if you go to a big bank, you are likely to be charged more fees than at a small bank. This is almost always true on services across the board, from a small checking account to big loans. When I was at the bank, they wanted a 3% loan origination fee and a document fee with every loan, even on loan renewals. We could often get the fees reduced, but not totally eliminated. My business partner and I recently bought a company and used a smaller bank. The loan origination fee was around 0.25% for a loan over a million dollars, we did not pay a documentation fee.

Even if the fee only adds up to a dollar or two per customer, if you have millions of customers, it adds up to big numbers. Is it fair? If you ask a national bank, they will say it is fair, and I think they have a point. Look at the extra technology they can offer—technology you cannot get at the local level. Even if the small bank charged a $1 fee, they would not have a large enough client base for those fees to fund expensive software and improved technology.

Just in case the big banks are feeling a little picked on in this chapter, I want to address one more thing. If your company does business internationally, seek out a bank with a department that specifically deals with foreign exchange. If you need this service, you are almost certain to need a larger bank. I ran into a business whose products were often manufactured in China, and they incurred a lot of expense by wiring money to China, not to mention that the owner prepaid for those products. This was inherently risky: what if the manufacturer did not ship the product? Was he going to go to China and track them down? Larger banks have sophisticated ways of transferring money internationally, as well as programs to protect you while doing business with foreign countries.

Bottom line with banks: they come in all different shapes and sizes. Ask questions! If you are a business owner, know your banker or branch manager. That way, if you have to call them, they will know you. Even big banks make judgment calls. If you own a larger business, and you do all your business with one bank, get to know *another* bank. Even if you do not do any business with them, it is important to have another resource, in case your relationship with your current bank goes south or they cannot fulfill your needs. When I was a business owner, I worked with two different banks and gave my financial information and tax returns to a third just in case I needed them.

Check Yourself:

- What are the advantages/disadvantages of small banks vs. big banks?
- Why does it make sense to ask a bank what types of loans they prefer to make?
- What other questions do you want to ask your banker?
- Why would you give your financial information to a bank that you are not currently using?

Chapter 7:

WHAT IS YOUR BANKABILITY?

If you went to a bank today and applied for a loan, would it get approved? If you are a business owner or individual who wants to buy a business, it is a good idea to have an idea of how bankable you are. Bankability refers to whether you can get a loan from a bank, and how much credit they are willing to give you. I am passionate about this subject because I had to learn these lessons the hard way. In my early days, I was told "no" a lot. I wish I had saved all the denial letters I received. Better yet, I wish I could rub them in a few people's noses!

A banker once told me that one of the reasons they did not want to give me a loan was because my company was growing too fast. What?! I thought that was the most ridiculous thing I had ever heard. At that point in my life, I did not know the meaning of the phrase *slow down*. My company was growing over 20% a year, and a couple of times we doubled our sales from one year to the next. When I went to work at the bank later in my life, sure enough, they also frowned on company growth over 20% year after year. So, what other crazy things can you expect from a bank during the underwriting or approval process?

Let's break this down. In its simplest terms, your bankability is determined by two things: cash flow and collateral. If I give you a loan, what kind of income or cash flow do you have to pay me back? And if you do not pay me back, what assets or collateral do you have that I can take to get my money back?

In its simplest terms, your bankability is determined by two things: cash flow and collateral.

We talked about cash flow in terms of valuing a company, but let's take another look at it. A bank will base 80% of their decisions around your cash flow from the past three years. If you go to the bank today, I guarantee they will ask for your last three years of tax returns and financial statements. So, if, in the last three years, your income has increased or stayed the same, that is good, and it gives them comfort that this trend will continue. This increases your bankability. If your income has decreased year over year or is up and then down, that is bad. Banks do not like inconsistencies in cash flow. If it is down year over year, they will assume it will keep going down. This decreases your bankability.

What about collateral? This is what secures the loan and what the bank gets if you do not pay them back. At the end of the day, the bank is probably more worried about cash flow, but the loan does have to be secured by some sort of collateral. What types of collateral do banks like? They like equipment or capital that holds value and can be easily converted to cash. I like to compare my oil company to farmers. Tri-County Petroleum was a cash cow. We generated a wealth of cash, but my collateral was terrible. No bank wants a bunch of gas tanks and petroleum bulk plants as collateral. It is all hazardous material, and who is going to buy a bulk plant if I do not pay the loan back? What are they going to do with hundreds of tanks I have leased out all over the countryside—if they could find them? A farmer, on the other hand, might not always have great cash flow because of low commodity prices or poor crop conditions, but they have excellent collateral, such as land, livestock, grain, and expensive farm equipment. All these things can be converted to cash very easily.

The other thing banks will do that will drive you crazy is discount your collateral. You may have a million dollars' worth of trucks, but they may only use 60% or 70% of that value. Why? There are a couple reasons, and it starts to make more sense when you think of it as the bank getting its money back. If they have to repossess that vehicle, it is probably a couple of years older than it was when the loan was made, so it is worth less now. They have to pay somebody to get it and then sell it, which may cost them 20% of the value of the vehicle. If they repossess it, that means you probably were not making any money and are likely not taking care of the vehicle, which makes it worth even less. But these are hard things to hear when you are the one trying to find more collateral for a loan.

Collateral was a huge problem with real estate in the last recession. If you bought real estate in 2007 right before the crash and your loan matured in five years, when you tried to renew that loan, it is quite possible that the value of the real estate was worth less than what was originally loaned on the property. That is called being upside down in a loan. The collateral is now worth less than the amount of the loan on the real estate. In this situation, banks commonly asked people to inject equity—or more collateral—or they asked you to pay the loan down with cash. If you could not do that, in many cases, they did not renew the loan. A lot of people lost their real estate, even though they never missed a payment. Think about what that did to their bankability.

Now let's make this a little more complicated. A bank wants a 20% down payment on a loan, or else they are going to look at how much equity you have in your company and your own personal net worth. The bank wants to see a debt service coverage ratio of 1.25. What is a debt service coverage ratio? That means they want to see that there is at least $1.25 in income from the company to cover every $1.00 worth of debt payments you have. So let's say your company has an income of $125,000 a year, and the loan you want had $80,000 per year in annual payments. If you divide $125,000 of income by $80,000 in debt payments, you get a debt service coverage ratio of 1.56, which means you have $1.56 in income for every $1 worth of debt. That is a bankable number that increases the possibility of getting that loan.

When you calculate your company's income, you add depreciation and amortization back to net income. These are non-cash expenses. You will also subtract any loan principal payments you have from current loans. Principal payments are cash that goes out of the company to pay down debt. That portion of your loan payment does not show up on your income statement— only the interest does. Make sense?

Let's assume you have a current loan payment of $1,000. If $200.00 of that loan payment is interest, interest expense shows up as an expense on your income statement. However, the $800.00 in principal only shows up on your balance sheet as a reduction in the amount of debt you still owe on the loan. When you understand this, you are at least 50% of the way to knowing your bankability. Today it is so simple to download something that will tell you what your loan payment will be, and you can figure this out very easily.

Let's take this one step further. It is very important for you to know what your *global debt service coverage ratio* is. We only added one word—*global*—which means the sum of all of your loan payments divided by all of your income. To do this, it is very helpful to have a debt schedule, and you will impress your banker if you present it to them before they ask for it.

It is so simple to create a debt schedule: it is just a spreadsheet where you have listed all of your loans. Show when the loan was originated, the original loan amount, the monthly payment amount, the interest rate, when the loan matures, and when is it scheduled to be paid off. If you have existing loans and want to secure another, add your proposed loan to the debt schedule, add your loan total together, and divide your total annual payments by your annual income. Are you still over 1.25?

Most of the time, if you own the company yourself, the bank will also want to see your personal loans on this schedule. Yes, that means the loan for your boat, your four-wheeler, both vehicles, and your house, etc. Good news! You get to add your spouse's income to your company's income. The debt schedule should be an eye opener. All those little things you bought because it was only $200 dollars a month add up. This is also a great way to see if it makes sense to consolidate a couple of loans to decrease your annual payments. Remember: the higher your debt service coverage ratio, the higher your bankability.

Most of the time, if you own the company yourself, the bank will also want to see your personal loans on this schedule.

What is an *amortization schedule*? Don't you love all these fancy words? Your amortization schedule is how long a bank will give you to pay the loan back. Typically, the amortization schedule is tied to how long that asset will be around. If you are buying a vehicle or piece of equipment or even a company, most of the time that amortization schedule will be five years. If you are buying a building, you could probably get twenty. There is a huge difference in loan payments between a truck loan for $250,000 that has an amortization schedule of five years and a building that could have an amortization schedule of twenty years. Download a loan calculator, write out your debt schedule, and look at what it does to your debt service coverage ratio. Then start playing with the numbers. Can consolidating some loans help improve your debt service coverage ratio? Do this before you go to the bank, and you will look very knowledgeable.

Now let's talk about your *balance sheet* and how much cash and equity you have in your company. Banks like to see cash on the balance sheet. How much cash? Divide your current assets by your current liabilities (your line of credit is a current liability). Is this a positive number? This is your current ratio. I would suggest targeting 1.5 – 2 for a current ratio. This tells the bank you have sufficient cash or assets to cover day-to-day expenses.

Banks like to see that the owner's equity portion is at least 20% of total assets. One thing that can be tricky, especially in today's world of bonus depreciation, is that you may have negative equity on your balance sheet. If you have purchased depreciable assets, you could outpace your income and have a negative equity position. You could also have assets that have appreciated in value since they were purchased, such as land or a building, which would undervalue the amount of true equity in the company. In both cases, I would create a balance sheet based on the market value of those assets and push your banker to use those values. They may not want to do that, but it is the true representation of equity in your company. The greater your current ratio and the more equity in your company, the greater your bankability.

There is a classic battle between your banker and your CPA. The banker wants to see a large amount of equity in your company. The only way to get equity on your balance sheet is to show profits on your income statement. If you show profits on your income statement, guess what? You have to pay taxes! So, guess what your CPA always tries to do? Find ways to reduce your profits, in order to minimize your taxes. This can almost become a game, but it is also why you must have these conversations with your banker to know what ratios they use to judge your company. If your ratios are in check, show as little profit as possible with the tools and methods that are legally available to you, and pay less in taxes. If your equity is upside down on your balance sheet—meaning you have negative equity—you may need to drive as much profit to the income statement as possible. This unfortunately means you will have to pay more taxes. But if you need money from the bank, you have to do what you can to make your financial statements show you as bankable.

The better you know and understand your bankability, the better decisions you will make about buying equipment or even your ability to do an acquisition. This is an important conversation to have with your CPA and banker. Ask your banker what key ratios they look at when considering a loan for your company. Then, ask your CPA to track those ratios monthly, just as you would your income statements or balance sheet.

As I mentioned at the beginning of the chapter, this is something that I am passionate about. With the oil company, I kept a rolling twelve-month worksheet for my income statement, balance sheet, and key ratios. Once you have the formulas in the worksheet, it is a piece of cake. I guarantee that your accountant or banker will be happy to help you get that set up.

Check Yourself:

- What does bankability mean?
- In its simplest form, what two things are considered for a loan?
- How many years of financial information does a bank typically want to make their decision?
- How much does a bank typically want for a down payment?
- What is typically a minimum debt service coverage ratio?
- What does global debt service coverage mean?
- What is the purpose of a debt schedule?
- Can you explain what an amortization schedule is?
- What is a classic battle between a CPA and a banker?

Chapter 8:

DO YOU NEED A FINANCIAL ADVISOR?

R ecently, I met with a financial advisor whose specialty is working with small businesses. He hit on some notes that I completely agreed with, and his thoughts were very similar to my own. His experience was that most small business owners do not have a lot of investable income, and they rely on the sale of their business for their retirement. This was true for me. While I owned the oil company, I did not have a lot of investable income because the money I made was funneled back into the company to provide capital and help it grow.

Maybe we should take a step back. What does a financial advisor do? I like to think of a CPA and a financial advisor as having two completely different focuses. A CPA reports what *has happened.* Yes, they can help with tax planning, which is something that can happen in the future, but they primarily report on your financial history. They cannot report something unless you sell something. By contrast, a financial advisor, is primarily concerned with what *will happen* in the future. What help do you need today to achieve your goals several years, decades even, into the future? How much money do you need to invest today or annually to meet your ultimate retirement goal?

Here is the tricky part: the team of financial advisors you need to help you when you have several million dollars is not going to work with you when you have less than $1 million of investable income. The types of investment products you need will change as you accumulate wealth—not only for your investable cash, but also for your real estate. I have often watched friends or clients start out with an advisor who is appropriate to help them with $50,000 to $500,000 of investable income. They become friends, form a long-term relationship, and when it is time for them to step up to the next level advisor, they cannot make the switch because they do not want to hurt their advisors' feelings.

... the team of financial advisors you need to help you when you have several million dollars is not going to work with you when you have less than $1 million of investable income.

So, what is the difference in needs? Think of it in percentages. The lower the amount you have to invest, let's say $50,000, the higher the percentage of people who have that same amount of money to invest. Naturally, there are more products out there for this type of investor. The more products available for those investors, the more salespeople you have for them.

Salespeople? I thought we were talking about financial advisors! Unfortunately, at this level, you have to remember that your financial advisor is really a salesperson who has goals to meet for his own financial gain. This person, unintentionally or not, will most likely sell you the financial products that meet their goals, but might not meet yours. As I write this, there are changes taking effect that require financial advisors to be more fiducially responsible with your money. New regulations are not always good, but there are some real problems with what people who call themselves "financial advisors" sell to investors at this level. Be diligent with your investments and ask questions. Do not fall in love with your advisor. You may need to make a break with this person as you move up the ladder of wealth.

Let's get back to our percentages. If you have over a million dollars to invest now, you are in what some people would call the 1% club. Welcome and congratulations! Less than 1% of the population will make it to this level. Now the level of expertise you need from a financial advisor changes dramatically. You need an advisor who can tailor a plan specifically to you. By now, you not only need advice on how to invest your money, but what to do with your company, real estate, gifts, taxes, etc. As I mentioned earlier, you get to a certain point in life and the question becomes not, how do I make more money, but rather, how do I keep Uncle Sam from getting what I have made? This is all part of the "You don't know what you don't know" problem.

The biggest hurdle can be at the turning point between having less than a million and over a million in investments is how you pay your advisor. When you cross that threshold, you will have to pay your advisor an annual fee based on the level of your investments, rather than transaction fees. For example, if you have between one and three million in investments, the fee may be in the ballpark of 1.25% annually.

To some people, this is the craziest thing they have ever heard. But like it or not, you have already been paying those fees (most likely at a higher rate). They were just hidden in the products you bought. That is the difference between loaded funds and unloaded funds. They were loaded with fees that you paid and probably did not know it. There are even different classes of stocks you can buy. This is not the place to describe all the differences, but it is important that you know there are differences and that you ask your advisor what they are.

People usually seek out a financial advisor to plan for retirement. We all want to retire, right? So, you start your 401K and plow as much money into it as possible. That is great. You will put untaxed dollars into an account that grows, and you will pull that money out at retirement when you are presumably in a lower tax bracket. A word of caution: If you are thinking about using that money to buy a business or to use as capital in your current business, don't. Yes, you can take it out, but there could be severe penalties for doing so.

There is a way to use your 401K money for a business purchase, but it is not easy. If you use your 401K money to buy a business, you have to set up a C-Corp, which in my opinion is a bad idea. Give this some serious thought. If you are willing to work a job for your entire career and you have no entrepreneurial ambitions, it is perfectly fine to put as much money as possible in that 401K. However, if you want that money to work for you as collateral or capital to buy or build a business, be cautious about stashing it away where it is hard to retrieve it.

You cannot use your 401K fund as collateral for a loan. It is called a non-qualified asset. When I worked at the bank, I saw some very upset people who had several hundred thousand dollars in their 401K account and wanted to use it as collateral. No dice.

I have never put my income into a retirement account because I always wanted to use that money to build my business. My business was my retirement account. The tricky part is, if your business is not successful, you do not have money to fall back on for your retirement!

The second most common goal people have is to put their children through college. Holy guacamole, I am at that place right now. This was my first year to receive two college bills and let me just say: Yikes! We thought we were being smart. We set up college accounts for all three of our children and put money into them since they were born. But we did not save enough, and it is painful. For millions of Americans, this may be as complicated as their financial life ever gets, other than maybe having a will to disperse their assets upon death. However, if you find yourself in the 1% club, life can get very complicated really fast, and you will need the help of a financial advisor that has access to a team of people to advise you.

You will probably need help with life insurance policies too, which could be an entire book on its own. All I can say is that there are several opinions, but the bottom line is: buyer beware. This is a financial product that salesmen will actively try to push on you, and there are big commissions that go to the salesman.

Trust accounts or irrevocable trust accounts are another thing to ask about. Make sure the real estate you own is set up in the correct name if you want to keep it or pass it on. It is sad to see a farm family forced to sell the land to pay for estate taxes. It is sad to see siblings who wanted to take over the family business but are forced to sell the business to pay for estate taxes. This is real stuff, and it happens all the time.

I have another saying which is, "Don't give this the ostrich treatment." Don't stick your head in the sand! You will need help to set these things up correctly. Do it right. Don't cheap out because you don't want to spend a nickel with an attorney. Saving a nickel will cost you thousands of dollars in the long run.

A big part of financial planning is estate planning. This is where the team concept really takes shape. How will you dispose of your business or pass it on to siblings or key employees? Does an Employee Stock Ownership Plan (ESOP) make sense? If you do not want or need all of the money from selling the company immediately, this could be a great option. What about gifting? Do you plan to give some of your money to a charity or foundation? As you can see, there is a lot to think about, and I have just begun to scratch the surface. The best advice I can give you is to seek out a professional and ask good questions.

I will be honest with you. I did not do any of these things before I sold the oil company. But I did not know what I did not know. I also did not want to tell someone what I was thinking while I was in the process. Fortunately, things turned out fine for me. Not perfectly, but fine. I definitely would do some things differently today. The big difference is that I now have a team of financial advisors in place. So, ask questions, and make the move up to the next level of advisor if needed. Do not be afraid to spend $10,000 to $15,000 to get your estate affairs in place. It could save you millions of dollars in the future.

Check Yourself:

- What does a typical small business do with the proceeds from the sale of their business?
- Can a financial advisor be a salesperson?
- Does it make sense that you would have the same financial advisor you had when you had $50,000 of investable income vs. $1 million?
- How does a financial advisor who manages over a million dollars get paid?
- What are the dangers of investing all your money in a 401K?
- What would be a wise thing to do before you sell your company?
- Your financial advisor should be a part of your _____?

Chapter 9:

HOW TO GET MAXIMUM VALUE FOR YOUR COMPANY

Another title for this chapter could be (and pardon my French) "Get your sh*t together!" If you want to get the maximum value for your company, you must be organized. You have to know what a buyer will want to see in your company and prove that yours will deliver.

We will start with the easiest one: good financial statements. Have them done in a timely manner and get your taxes done on time. I am currently working with a client who wants to sell his business. It is the middle of September, and he still does not have his taxes done from last year. It is driving me crazy! And it will drive a potential buyer crazy, too—enough to send him or her running the other direction. This is one of the first things you will be asked for when you are ready to sell your business: three to five years of financial statements and your tax returns. If you produce them immediately, you will look better and the whole process will flow smoothly.

Other ways you to improve the value of your company surround the business process. Do you have a management team in place who can run the company if you are not there? Do you have non-compete clauses with your employees? Does the company have recurring income? Are your customers under long-term contracts? What have you done to ensure that when you sell the business those customers will continue to do business with the new owner? Let's break these questions down.

Day-to-Day Management

Do you have to be there to run the day-to-day operations? If not, your company has intrinsically higher value. I have talked about a number of things that I think I did well, as well as things I should have done differently. This is one thing I really nailed. My company would have run just fine if I was not there. I managed the company, but my management team ran it. I had three operations managers and an office manager and, quite frankly, they were probably happier when I just let them do their job. Because they were good at their jobs! To any prospective buyer, having a management team in place that does a great job is a winner, winner chicken dinner, my friend. This will help bring a maximum value for your company. I run into way too many companies where, if the owner is gone, there is no one there to lead the charge or manage the business.

Even if you do not need to be there, what is in place to keep your key employees there if you sell the company? It is wise to have non-compete clauses with your employees, although that is a touchy thing to introduce to long-term employees. One way to handle this is to rewrite the employee manual and include it as an addition. When you hand out the new manual, get everyone to sign that they have read and agreed to it. In addition, owners often use an insurance policy that builds in cash value and then returns that cash value to the employees, but only if they stay with the company. This is commonly known as the golden handcuffs.

Do you have job descriptions and SOPs (standard operating procedures)? When you have these in place, it is easier to replace an employee. A new employee should be able to step into any position in the company and have some sort of manual or SOP to guide them through the day-to-day functions of that position.

What about the assets of the company? Do you have a list of them? Do you know where they are? These may sound like silly questions, but you would be surprised. I had twenty-plus trucks, several trailers, hundreds if not over a thousand tanks and pumps out in the country that were leased to customers. We had a three-ring binder for each vehicle that included maintenance records, a copy of the title, etc. Every item was detailed. All our equipment that was out in the country had signed lease agreements. That is critical. If you want to sell an asset that is on someone else's property and you do not have a signed lease agreement, there will be questions about who really owns the equipment, or if the customer quits, how you will get it back?

You need to have a detailed list of the equipment that will be sold with the company. The buyer will want to see this. For one thing, they may need an equipment appraisal as part of their loan package. The more detailed information you can give them provided in a timely manner, the more your company value will increase.

And who owns all of this stuff? You do, right? Yes, but do you know what entity has title to it? Again, if you have a larger company, and you own several properties with different assets, are they all in one name? Is some of the "stuff" in your personal name or under separate LLCs? You need to have all of this organized. It will make things go so much smoother. The smoother it goes, the easier it is for someone to make an offer. I have literally seen situations where the paperwork was such a disaster, that the buyer threw out a low-ball number out with the attitude that if the seller takes it, we will help them figure it out.

Think about your business and how it runs. What skill sets need to be replaced when you exit the company? What is the depth of knowledge each of your employees contribute to the business? What will change when you are not there? Be prepared to tell a potential buyer exactly how things flow, and why this would be a piece of cake for them to step right in and continue the work you have done for years. There is nothing wrong with being upfront; tell them where you think you excel and where you would make improvements. There might be something new they can bring to the table.

Now about equipment and the assets that are used to create the cash flow of the company. I am selling a small trucking company right now that just bought two new trucks, and they have a total of seven trucks. They borrowed the money to buy the trucks because they had to replace two older ones that were shot. Now they have added debt to their balance sheet, equal to about 20% of the purchase price of the company, which is based on their cash flow. Those two new trucks are not likely to increase the cash flow of the company, but they will ensure that it maintains that cash flow. Sadly, they did not increase the value of the company, and they definitely decreased the amount of cash they will pocket after the sale because they will have to pay off the loan on those two trucks.

What is the moral of this story? Unless you are a 100% service-based operation, your assets were purchased to create cash flow for the company. If you plan to sell the business, those assets should be in good operating order to continue generating cash flow. You need to think ahead to find a balance between having solid assets to continue to generate cash flow, and not borrowing too much money for new assets right before you decide to sell. I have bought companies knowing that I would not be able to use any of their rolling stock because it was junk. That was reflected in the price I paid for the company. We bought one company that only had one delivery truck, and the driver's seat was so shot that the driver used an old set of coveralls as the seat cushion. That is not good.

Unless you are a 100% service-based operation, your assets were purchased to create cash flow for the company. If you plan to sell the business, those assets should be in good operating order to continue generating cash flow.

We started this chapter with financial statements, so we might as well end with them as well. Everything we have talked about in this chapter will help you maximize the value of your company, which is ultimately derived from your cash flow over the last three to five years.

The most important year is the last year, then the year before that, etc. What does that trend look like? If it goes up, perfect. If it is flat, okay. If it goes down, bad, bad, bad. I see too many businesses that should have sold three years earlier, but now they are on that glider path, which I mentioned in an earlier chapter. Sales and revenue have been sliding down year after year, just like the owner's interest. If you want to maximize the value of your company, kick butt in the last three years before you sell it. You might have to pay some income taxes, but if you do things right and add $100,000 to the bottom line, you could increase the value of your company by as much as $400,000. Do not do business under the table. I always say, "You cannot sell the wink!" Clean up your finances, cut expenses, and rock it.

Do not fool yourself. The person who wants to buy your company wants it to make money. If you want to maximize the value of your company, make that old penny look like a shiny new dime, and be prepared to show any potential buyer why you think this business will make them 25% to 30% on their investment.

Check Yourself:

- If someone wants to buy a company, how many years of financial information will they typically ask for?
- Describe the importance of a good management team.
- What is recurring revenue?
- Why is it important to have a non-compete clauses in your employee agreement?
- What is the danger of purchasing an expensive asset right before you sell a company?
- Why is it hard to sell the "wink?"
- Ultimately, the value of a company is derived from what?

Chapter 10:

YOU BUILT IT! NOW WHAT?

So, you have spent the majority of your life—or at very least a significant amount of time—building your business. Then one day this thought sneaks into your mind: *What do I do with this business when I no longer want to do this business? How do I get out of it?* If selling your business is a major source of your retirement, will it be worth what you need to retire? If it is, how do you get from where you are now to depositing that big, fat check?

This is where all the elements in this book come together. Business valuation, financial statements, bankers, attorneys, financial advisors, business brokers, and building that team of people are critical to help bring you to the finish line. One of your first steps will be to value the company. This must be done by someone other than Uncle Bob's brother's friend's neighbor who sold a lemonade stand one time. Work with a professional! Who is on your team? Talk to your CPA or ask your attorney to recommend someone who is qualified to give you a realistic value. Better yet, just call me.

I am a CVA (Certified Valuation Analyst). A CVA assesses the cash flow of a business to determine its approximate value. As a CVA, I can tell you it is absolutely critical to have a realistic expectation of what your business is worth. This is one of the most essential steps in selling your business. If the price is overstated, you will waste a lot of people's time and energy.

I run into this all the time. I am working with a company right now, and I have brought them several willing and able buyers, but I cannot get it through the owner s head that the company is overpriced. Here is the thing: you cannot sell a company for its future potential. Sellers often say, "Someone could buy this company, and with a little more marketing or by adding one piece of equipment, they could make a fortune." Potential does not equal a higher sales price. It does not work that way. You have to assess the current value, not any potential future value. And if things could improve with a tweak or two, why didn't you do it yourself?

Let's assume we have determined a realistic value. Who would want to buy it, and how do we find that person? Even tougher is, how do we find that person and keep it confidential? This is really one of the trickiest aspects of the whole process. You want to sell your business, but you do not want anyone to know that it is for sale. In a perfect world, you have already found the perfect buyer and have worked on the transition plan for some time. Unfortunately, this is rarely the case.

You want to sell your business, but you do not want anyone to know that it is for sale.

Look for the low hanging fruit first. Is there a family member or key employee who might want to buy the business? Do you have a friendly competitor who might be interested? Those are all good places to start. If they are interested, there are some simple steps you can take. First, find someone will work for you on an hourly basis to be an intermediary between you and the buyer. This could be a business broker or attorney. It can make the process more comfortable than if you tried to work out all the details face to face, and I have always had success with this approach. When you work with a professional who knows the process, you can vet out your questions in a less awkward manner. That person should be able to help you determine if your questions or concerns are valid.

What if you do not find an intermediary or you do not feel comfortable pursuing those people yourself? Go back to your team. It is completely acceptable—even recommended—to tell your banker, attorney, or financial advisor that you want to sell your company. Oddly enough, your insurance person is also a good person to ask, especially if your type of insurance is industry specific. You should have confidence that these team players will keep your desires confidential. In the fuel and lubricants business, there were only two predominant insurance carriers, and my insurance broker dealt with many other oil companies. He always knew who was interested in expanding.

Business Brokers

Your other option is to work with a business broker. Out of all the companies I have purchased, I have never used a business broker. However, I did sell my oil company through a broker, and it was a positive experience. At one point, I tried to buy a company through a broker, and it was a disaster. I felt like chum in shark-infested waters. They had me so confused that I finally walked away from the deal. I eventually bought the company two years later on my own. For the seller in this case, using the broker obviously did not work. Having said that, a major part of my work is brokering businesses, and we successfully sell companies this way because we are good at finding buyers.

What should you expect from a broker? Their fee will be between 8% and 12% if your company is worth less than $1 million. The higher the value of the company, the lower the fee should be. We just listed a company worth $8 to $10 million and our fee is 5% up to $8 million, and 3% for anything over that. It is not unusual to have a sliding fee on large deals. On deals under $1 million, a $500 to $1,000 marketing fee is standard, and hopefully the broker will deduct that fee off of their commission if the company is sold. If the company does not sell, the fee is not refundable.

On larger deals, it is not unusual to pay your broker a monthly fee. On the deal I just mentioned, we are paid $2,500 per month, and the total amount they pay us will be deducted from our commission when the company sells. Again, those fees are non-refundable. The fees and commissions are all negotiable. I have heard of firms that charge $5,000 per month *plus* the commission, and the monthly fees are not deducted on the back side.

Some firms will charge you a fee on the sale price of the company, as well as on the inventory. I do not do that in my practice, and I did not pay a fee on my inventory when I sold the oil company. It is not unusual to be charged if the broker negotiates a lease for real estate that the owner may keep. You also want to be aware of what is called *the hook*. The hook is how long the broker will receive fees for the sale of your company after the brokerage agreement expires. My agreement states that I will receive my fee if a company or individual that I showed the company to buys it up to twenty-four months after the agreement expires and six months if anyone else buys it. Personally, I think that is fair, although I have seen contracts where that six months is three to five years. I do not like that. The bottom line for using a broker is that he or she should bring you a qualified buyer in a reasonable amount of time.

Confidentiality

We touched on this before. It is important and complicated to keep the sale of your business confidential. How do you sell the business if you cannot tell anyone it is for sale? If your employees find out the company is for sale, they may quit. You may lose customers. If your competitors find out your company is for sale, they may start calling on your customers, which really fires up the rumor mill. Once the cat is out of the bag, it spreads like wildfire. The more people involved in the sale of the company, the harder it is to control that information.

If your employees find out the company is for sale, they may quit. You may lose customers. If your competitors find out your company is for sale, they may start calling on your customers, which really fires up the rumor mill.

When I sold the oil company, it was actually sold to nine different companies. As I mentioned earlier, one of the managers sent an email out to all of his employees prematurely that announced that they were buying my company. By the end of that day, the rumor mill was in full swing. Employees were asking questions. Customers were calling. It was a nightmare. We were fortunate the company sold a couple of weeks after that, but it could have been disastrous. Had the company not sold, this situation could have ended in a lawsuit. It is important to think this through and make sure you do not use a common email for the whole company. I have been bitten by that one. I once sent an email to the owner and did not know that everyone in the office checked that email as well.

Sometimes confidentiality can bite you the other way. I was working with the owner of a shooting range who was really concerned about confidentiality. He would not let us market it to anyone within a twenty-five miles radius. After a year, he let us loosen the reins of confidentiality, so to speak, and we found a prospect who owned a gun shop not ten miles from the shooting range. This guy would have bought it in a heartbeat because he wanted a shooting range, but he had just purchased another building a month earlier and did not have the capacity to purchase this, too.

In terms of the sale, much of the process is the same as it is when you buy a company, except the shoe is now on the other foot. The most important thing is that you use your business acumen and common sense. Hopefully you are in a position where you can vet out who is buying your company and find out if that person's business skills are acceptable to you! This is especially true if you have employees that you are legitimately concerned about.

We recently sold a company where we had two identical offers. The owner chose one buyer over the other strictly because he thought that man would be a better fit with his employees and his legacy. If you are in a position where you do not have to sell, you have every right to say, "No, I don't want to sell to my company to this buyer." But if the company is your competitor or is already in your market, obviously they now know that you are for sale, which could create other problems. So, if you work with a broker, it is important to tell them who you will not sell to. You can also ask to approve any interested party before they send them information that discloses the name of your company.

There are some additional things to think about when you find a buyer. First, are they capable of buying the company? In other words, are they bankable? In one situation, I was asked to be the intermediary between the buyer and seller. The seller asked me to help them through the process. They had found the buyer and wanted us to help them through the process. Perfect. Or so we thought. We got all the way down to the closing when we found out that the buyer was completely unbankable, which was frustrating to both me and the seller.

If the purchase will be a merger with another company, is there a difference in company culture? Will your employees stay on? When I sold my oil company, I knew there were huge differences in our company cultures, but I also knew that every employee would be able to keep their job and would end up with a much better benefit plan than I could ever offer.

Depending on your business model, you may have to vet out if your supplier will sell to the person or company trying to buy yours. If they will not, there probably will not be a deal.

And finally, how much do you care about what happens to your company after you sell? This includes your employees, vendors, the CPA, your bank, your real estate, et cetera. It is actually not your responsibility to make sure that everyone is happy about the sale. In fact, when you sell your business, especially if it is a moderate size, it will create a lot of heartache for you and many others. Prepare yourself with the mental fortitude it takes to make it through this process, as painful and necessary as it may be.

The best advice I can give you is to rely on your team. If you look back through the previous chapters of this book and follow through on what I have suggested, you should feel completely confident moving forward with the team of people you have built around you.

Once the paperwork is in process and you know the deal is secure, you can start letting your vendors, employees, and others know that change is coming. Letting your customers know can be a little trickier. When I bought the other oil companies, the day we took possession, we sent out a thank-you letter from the previous owner to all the customers that recommended they stick with us. We also sent a letter from our company that welcomed them and told them how happy we were to service them as a new customer. We mailed both letters in the same envelope.

I also went with the previous owner to personally visit the largest customers, explain the transition, and answer any questions they had. This enabled us to retain about 95% of the customer base. If we could get out to see the customer before a competitor found out about the acquisition, we were very successful and kept those accounts.

This was a situation where the new company had a different name, and the corporate transition would be highly visible. But maybe you are buying a company and are not changing the name, or the customers really will not notice that there has been a change. We recently purchased a property management company and kept the same name and the same employees. We told a few people, but for the most part, the customers never really knew there was a change in ownership. Every situation is different.

The final question is how long should the previous owner stay around? I have had several situations where the previous owner stayed on and worked for me for several years, but this is unusual. Generally, the previous owner sticks around and is available at no charge to the buyer for three months. The first week will be very busy, but in the second week, things settle down and take shape. By the third week, the previous owner should only have to be around the office occasionally or be available for some meetings and to answer questions by phone. In most situations, by the third month the previous owner is not needed.

For the last company we purchased, my partner wanted to negotiate a year-long contract with a substantial amount of money to be paid to the seller. I said, "Trust me, in three months, everything will be fine." Instead, we agreed to pay the owner an hourly consultation fee after three months. Six weeks after the acquisition, the owner went on a two-week vacation. Upon return, the previous owner cleaned out their office and that was that. Later, we did use the previous owner on a project and paid some money for the work, but the three-month transition went just fine.

During the process, I like to tell employees and customers alike to, "Keep an open mind. Everyone usually wants to do the right thing, we will work through this, and it will all work out fine. Keep an open mind."

Check Yourself:

- What is the first thing you should do when you get ready to sell your business?
- What is the number one deal killer in selling a company?
- Who would be considered as low hanging fruit for potential buyers of your company?
- Who might a business owner consider working with to sell their company?
- What are some things to be aware of when signing a contract with a business broker?
- How important is confidentiality?
- How long does a previous owner typically stay around after the sale of the business?
- What is a good thing to say to employees and customers as you go through the process of selling a business?

Chapter 11:

DON'T BE THE DOG
THAT CAUGHT THE CAR!

did not do a very good job of using my team when I sold my business. I kept confidential information from them for too long. Obviously, my attorney was involved early on, and he did a great job. But I did not tell my accountant until the very end, which upset him, and I probably would have had a much better tax situation had I involved him early on. I did not seek the advice of a financial advisor either. To be honest, I did not even know what to look for. My total personal investments amounted to less than $80,000 at that point. My company was my retirement vehicle. It was only dumb luck that it all worked out.

I never thought about what I was going to do with myself after I sold the business. I agreed to work for the buyer for six months after the purchase. After that, they could continue to employ me, or we could part ways. When the six months was up, we amicably parted ways, which was funny because in the beginning, they said they wanted me and my company because they could not understand how efficient we were. But at the end of the day, they decided to keep doing things their own way. Here I was, just forty years old, and I literally had no idea what the heck to do with the rest of my life.

My wife was tickled pink. Our kids were ten, twelve, and fourteen at the time, so she got to do exactly what she wanted to do, which was to be a full-time mom. She had worked for me in the business, and I told her that if we sold, she would not have to work anymore.

On the other hand, I had just gone from running a seven-day-a-week company with over $42 million in sales, three thousand customers, and twenty-three employees to . . . absolutely nothing. Which is exactly what I wanted, right? I went from answering fifty to sixty calls a day to looking at my phone and wondering if it still worked.

It was great for about a month. Hunting season had just started, so I spent a lot of time in the woods, and I had time to help a buddy build a new shed at the farm. Then reality started to set in. I thought, *I can only hunt and piddle so much. What the heck am I going to do with myself?* I watched *The Today Show* in the morning, *The Price Is Right* at noon, and *Oprah* in the afternoon. That is all cool at first, but soon I was bored to tears. Then there was my wife. It did not take long for her to get tired of me being around the house. Apparently, our house is a marital asset that she does not want me to inhabit in the daytime!

I never thought about what I was going to do with myself after I sold the business....Then there was my wife. It did not take long for her to get tired of me being around the house. Apparently, our house is a marital asset that she does not want me to inhabit in the daytime!

Don't be like the dog that caught the car! If you are accustomed to going a hundred miles per hour, when you slow down to ten, while refreshing at first, it can get real boring real fast. In addition, I went from being the king, the top of the heap, Mr. President to the average Joe. Now there was a big change in how people treated me, from former customers to former employees, to former vendors. Notice how everything has the word *former* in front of it.

A lot of vendors were mad at me. I had a pretty big company, and they made a lot of money from it. In addition, we were headquartered in a small town that received plenty of money generated from the sales tax from my company. That was now gone. I laugh about this because I had never given any thought to the amount of tax revenue my company generated for that town, and now that revenue was gone. I laugh because they sure as heck did not do anything special for me while the company was there. These were definitely some unexpected twists after I sold the company.

My age was also a big factor. I was only forty years old. If you are sixty-five, I think it would be much different. Or would it? Maybe you planned to buy a lake house, but if you did not plan it through with your financial advisor or your CPA, the tax consequences might be worse than you thought and now having that lake house could be a strain on the budget. When I sold the company, one of the last things I agreed to was that I would keep all the real estate. That was a bad idea! I did not know anything about real estate. It was April of 2010, and we were in the middle of a huge recession. Not only did I have real estate in a declining market, but I also still had bills to pay from those properties. Insurance, property taxes, electric, and water were expenses that kept coming after the company sold.

Here is something else that sounds so obvious that it is easy to forget: you sold the company. You killed that goose! Make sure you have a conversation with your financial advisor because that paycheck just stopped. It really does take a team to get you through the process and, seriously, you don't know what you don't know. Build that team, rely on their expertise, and you will avoid a lot of potholes.

What do you do when the phone no longer rings? The sun still comes up every morning, and you have some days to fill. I was President of my Rotary Club the first year, which kept me busy. I had a chance to go to the Rotary International Convention, which was fantastic. Twenty thousand Rotarians in one place!

One day my phone did ring. It was someone from the big bank, who wanted to know if I wanted to work as a commercial lender. Being a kid from a small town of six hundred people, I always thought it would be fun to work for a big company. They offered me a good salary, great benefits, and my wife was happy about it, so I took the job. Going to work every day with a tie on made me feel a bit like a pig in heels, but I got used to it. The experience was great and painful—at the same time.

When I started, the bank was very structured. It was interesting, and there was no thinking outside of the box. My job was to follow the rules. At first this was refreshing because I was tired of making and enforcing rules. I learned a ton—so many questions I'd had as a business owner were finally answered. Do they look at net income or cash flow? How do they evaluate and consider collateral? Just learning the process of loan underwriting was beneficial. It was also helpful to hear a bank's side of the story. Big shock: there was usually a good reason for their rules, and they usually revolved around a previous process that burned them in some way. I liked to tell my clients that I had been involved in banking for over twenty years, just not on this side of the fence.

After three and a half years, my entrepreneurial itch came back, and that tie had started to feel like a noose! By this time, I'd had a lot of time to reflect. It seems that you forget about the bad stuff first. All the weekends and late nights, all the worry, all the pain-in-the-butt customers. I did not really miss the company, and anytime I started to regret selling, all I had to do was call up one of my former operations managers to be reminded of why I did not want that job anymore.

But there were two things I did miss: my fun equipment and my maintenance guy, Tommy. Tommy could fix anything, and I have to admit, it was kind of cool having forklifts, boom trucks, and pick-up trucks with lift gates at my disposal. What it really came down to was my time. I discovered that I really do like to work, but I wanted to work on my own time. I did not want to work an eight to five job, and I did not want to be available 24/7 either.

I asked myself what would really made me happy. What did I enjoy? I knew the answer. It was buying other companies. That was more fun than running the oil company. I missed going out to talk to other business owners, planting that seed and then negotiating the deal, buying the company, and merging it into ours. I missed meeting new people and finding new opportunities. In fact, when I sold my company, I had a deal worked to buy another one if the sale did not go through. When I started thinking about selling my company, the first thing I did was get someone to value it. When they told me the figure, I said, "If you can get that for it, sell it!" What I should have done was talk to my financial advisor, but you don't know what you don't know, right?

The idea of helping other people to buy, sell, and value companies began to settle in my bones. I earned my CVA (Certified Valuation Analyst) designation through the National Association of Certified Valuation Analyst or NACVA. I also teamed up with my partner, Dave Kunkel, and we started Innovative Business Advisors. Dave owns a commercial real estate company and had come across real estate deals where the company was also for sale. I have known Dave from high school, and when we were re-introduced by a mutual friend, we started Innovative Business Advisors from scratch. That is how I know how difficult it is to start a company from scratch, as I mentioned in chapter one. Our goal is to help people buy and sell companies. We also do business valuations and consulting work.

Along the way, I have learned that selling companies is hard, and selling small companies is *really* hard. One of my bucket list items has always been to write a book, and everything I have written in this book will help you to buy or sell a business. What I have learned has come through the school of hard knocks. I truly appreciate the saying, "You don't know what you don't know," and my goal is to pass on what I have learned, so you don't have to go through all the knocks the way I did.

Selling the oil company was one of the hardest decisions of my life, but my life is a lot simpler and less stressful now. I love to work, and I love to help people. I am sure there is still so much that I don't know, but now that I know what I do know, what the heck, let's do it again!

I hope my wife doesn't kill me!

Check Yourself:

- What did Terry fail to do before he sold his company?
- Why is it important to plan for life after you sell your business?
- How important is it to make sure you have a solid financial plan for your income after the sale of the company?
- What are some advantages/disadvantages of selling your company?
- What is one of the most important things to do to avoid the pitfalls of buying or selling a business?
- Who should you have on your team?

ABOUT THE AUTHOR

Terry Lammers grew up watching his parents run their own company in the fuel & lubricants industry, and eventually came on as a full-time employee in the early 90's and took over as President of the company.

In just 18 years, Tri-County Petroleum had purchased 11 different companies, growing Terry's family business from $750,000 annual sales to over $42 million when the company was sold in 2010.

Today, as Co-Founder and Managing Member of Innovative Business Advisors, Terry taps into his financial expertise and hands-on business experience to advise and guide business owners who are interested in learning the value of their business, the process of acquiring new businesses, or knowing when and how to sell their business.

Terry received his designation as a Certified Valuation Analyst (CVA), which is an accreditation through the National Association of Certified Valuation Analysts (NACVA).

In Terry's book, *You Don't Know What You Don't Know™: Everything You Need to Know to Buy or Sell a Business*, he provides an in-depth examination of the process of buying, growing, and eventually selling a business. No matter what stage of business ownership you're in, Terry will help you understand how to navigate the twists and turns of the business cycle and steer your enterprise toward success.

Terry also currently serves as the CFO for Banner Fire Equipment, Inc. in Roxana, IL and Chickasha, OK. Banner is a leading supplier of fire apparatus, equipment and service.

Email: terry@innovativeba.com

https://www.linkedin.com/in/terry-lammers-cva-b02b996/

https://youdontknowwhatyoudontknow.com/

www.businessprofitimprovementplan.com

A free ebook edition is available with the purchase of this book.

To claim your free ebook edition:

1. Visit MorganJamesBOGO.com
2. Sign your name CLEARLY in the space
3. Complete the form and submit a photo of the entire copyright page
4. You or your friend can download the ebook to your preferred device

Morgan James
BOGO™

A **FREE** ebook edition is available for you
or a friend with the purchase of this print book.

CLEARLY SIGN YOUR NAME ABOVE

Instructions to claim your free ebook edition:
1. Visit MorganJamesBOGO.com
2. Sign your name CLEARLY in the space above
3. Complete the form and submit a photo
   of this entire page
4. You or your friend can download the ebook
   to your preferred device

Print & Digital Together Forever.

Snap a photo   Free ebook   Read anywhere